Called to Manage

A Spiritual Guide to Workplace Leadership

A.M. Simmons

Copyright © 2020 All rights reserved

ISBN: 9798589445787

HTTPS://CalledToManage.com

ACKNOWLEDGEMENTS

I am blessed with my wife of thirty-eight years and counting. She has supported me throughout my career and college education. She is a mentor and role model in my spiritual journey. She has supported me with my writing and has tirelessly read countless re-writes.

Thanks to my editor, Catherine, who provided wonderful suggestions and edits to this manuscript. Thanks to Dave and Terry who also proofread my manuscript and gave me insight, suggestions, and much encouragement.

I am thankful to God and try to be a steward of everything He has entrusted to me. This includes the knowledge I have accumulated over my years of management so that I could write this book. God is good!

BIBLICAL REFERENCES

(GNT)
Scripture quotations marked (GNT) are from the Good News Translation in Today's English Version- Second Edition Copyright © 1992 by American Bible Society. Used by Permission.

(ERV)
Taken from the HOLY BIBLE: EASY-TO-READ VERSION © 2014 by Bible League International. Used by permission.

(GW)
Scripture is taken from GOD'S WORD®, © 1995 God's Word to the Nations. Used by permission of Baker Publishing Group.

(BBE)
The Bible In Basic English was printed in 1965 by Cambridge Press in England. Public Domain in the United States.

CONTENTS

Introduction 7

PART 1: Your Purpose
    Chapter 1: Spiritual Alignment 15
    Chapter 2: What Does Your Name Stand For 21
    Chapter 3: What Is Your Purpose 31

PART 2: Your Plan
    Chapter 4: Accountable to Yourself 41
    Chapter 5: Accountable in Your Relationships 49
    Chapter 6: Accountable in Managing Others 57
    Chapter 7: Decisions and Wise Counsel 71
    Chapter 8: What Is Your Plan 81

PART 3: Your Action
    Chapter 9: Overwhelmed 89
    Chapter 10: Get Help and Manage 101
    Chapter 11: Managing Up vs. Politics 109
    Chapter 12: Take Action 119

Summary and Conclusion
    Chapter 13: Summary and Conclusion 129
    Afterward: Life Beyond Managing 135

Appendix: Rules in Olde English 145

Bibliography 162

Introduction

Are you a manager of people? Well, my educational background is not typical for authoring a book on management. Then again this is not a book on business strategy for C-level executives and upper management. This book is not written to the level of a doctoral thesis which would require substantial study and time to understand the content. It is not a condensed graduate class in management. Instead, the subject matter within these pages is targeted for a critical element of every business: *people managers*. The content within this book utilizes on-the-job practical experience rather than textbook knowledge. The reason for this is that I have no graduate degree or MBA. In fact, I *squeezed* my undergraduate business degree into twenty-three-years! The content is primarily derived from experience learned from the school of "hard knocks." These experiences come from managing people for more than 30 years and is the foundation from which this book is written. Also unusual for a business management book is my emphasis on the spiritual aspect of managing people. This is thoroughly integrated into this book as well for the specific purpose of helping you perceive and evaluate your role as a manager of people as a spiritual calling.

CALLED TO MANAGE

My schooling of "hard knocks" began at age nineteen when I managed a convenience store with only a handful of employees to staff it 24-hours a day, seven days a week. On a regular basis someone would call in or just not show up at all. So, I learned to make quick decisions in order to cover shifts, otherwise I would have to work a double shift. After almost five years of managing convenience stores, I moved to managing an electronics retail store. Managing an electronics store lasted for only a year, leading to the discovery that not everyone is cut out for a career in sales. Next, I managed in the automotive service industry for about seven years. At some point, most people will experience a major upheaval in their career. When that happens, it can be a very difficult change. It can also be the most beneficial change in one's career. For me it led to joining a Fortune 500 company where I have managed for more than twenty years.

Every workplace needs strong and caring people managers so that we keep our businesses strong and competitive in the world's marketplace. Companies often talk about placing a lot of importance on great people managers, but the truth is that management is filled with human beings who are not perfect. You will hear about how imperfect decisions and other factors have led to a proliferation of installing poor, weak, or inadequate people managers. One of the most common reasons that employees leave a company is due to their managers. Often the people that leave a business this way are those that are talented and find other opportunities easily, leaving behind a diluted talent pool that has lost some exceptional talent.

CALLED TO MANAGE

A strong and caring manager should be committed to something greater than themselves. From a spiritual standpoint, you might not be called to preaching or missionary work as a vocation. However, spiritual beliefs may influence your decisions regarding your vocation. We are all called to be a Godly role-model in our everyday life. Have you thought that the job you have is where God wanted you to be? Have you thought about what God wants you to do and more importantly how you can serve the people around you, role-modeling a Godly Life? If we live for God, we are on a journey of faith and it does not stop when you walk into the door of your business. Your work life is an important part of your spiritual walk, and we are expected to be Christ-like wherever we are. Not only are we to build up and support the Church Body, our friends, and our family, but we are called to build up and support others in the workplace. In all aspects of our life, whether in work or relationships, we are directed to act in a Godly way.

As managers of people, I believe that we are called to serve and support our direct reports and our entire team (the term "Direct reports" is related to the employees reporting directly to their immediate manager). We must seek to help them be successful in their job and career, leading and managing them in a Godly way. Biblical-based management can be transformational and as a result you may see and experience a new strength and productivity in your team. I believe that when managers work to transform themselves, their entire team will also flourish. Their business will see growth, gains in efficiency, and profitability. I feel called to relate my experience and share God's great love for people to other managers and future managers. There is a need to transform people management, and in this book I will share my beliefs about managing people well.

In Europe, the eighteenth century was considered the Age of Enlightenment due to the advancements in many areas from science to exploration, including the advancement of business knowledge. Business leaders collaborated more, and an increased accumulation of knowledge was evident. One example of this was the groups of like businesses that formed guilds and associations. As a result, there is a fascinating eighteenth-century book published by one of these guilds entitled, *Some rules for the conduct of life: to which are added, a few cautions, for the use of such freemen of London, as take apprentices.* Within this book there are 35 rules on the conduct for managing their personal, spiritual, and business lives. They collaborated to develop guidelines for living your best life.

Again and again, it is amazing to see that the Bible contains a wealth of knowledge that is relevant today. We can see that human nature has not changed since Adam and Eve. Similarly, these business rules were written in the 1700s and we see that human nature in the workplace has not changed. These 35 rules are the foundation for this book, many of which include an embedded scripture. I have translated the rules into our current language and have updated the scriptures using modern translations of the Bible to improve readability and comprehension. The translation is from a copy of an

Olde English manuscript and because some parts were faded or illegible, the translation may not be perfect. Here is a typical example of an Olde English rule and the book's modern interpretation:

Olde English: Rule X
"Take care to fix right principles well in your mind; for want of which men are often inconsistent and unsteady in their actions, and uneasy to themselves and others. And when you have well fixed your principles, be sure always to speak and act according to them; and never to vary from them for the sake of party, or any other worldly consideration. For thus doing, God, your own conscience, and good men, will approve you: And you ought not to be moved at the censures of fools or wicked men."

Translation: Rule 10
Establish a firm set of beliefs, otherwise you may be inconsistent in word and action causing others to question you. This includes, not compromising your beliefs for personal gain or to benefit others. In doing this, you will find confidence in yourself, you will find approval from others, and approval from God. Do not listen to those who are reckless or corrupt.

The Olde English book begins with three rules that establish the overall structure for success in business, and the remaining 32 rules are related to "how" you get there. For the first rule, a corporation might refer to it as a mission statement or a vision, but a person of faith might call it their **purpose**. The second rule relates to how you should work towards your goals or purposes that were just mentioned and develop a **plan** in each area of your life. This plan should include how you are going to achieve each of your goals and milestones, and how the plan aligns with your overall purpose. The third rule is about **taking action** and not getting stuck in analysis paralysis, or in planning something to death, but to pick yourself up and get to work. These three rules form a simple outline to **identify your purpose**, **create your plan**, and **take action**. Whether you are beginning your journey or if circumstances are bringing about a "reset" in your life, these principles and rules will help you move forward.

As you proceed through the book, each chapter will stand by itself with its own content and subject matter. The chapters will include various rules created and compiled by the business leaders of eighteenth-century London. In its entirety, the book seeks to provide a number of helpful and relative lessons of wisdom for you, the frontline manager. The titles of "manager" and "leader" are used throughout this book, referring to those individuals who manage and lead their team in whatever capacity.

PART 1: Your Purpose

CALLED TO MANAGE

Chapter 1:
Spiritual Alignment

Where do we start regarding this unique book on management? We start on our first priority in life which is our spiritual condition. This chapter includes four rules from the Olde English book that encourages us to examine our spiritual condition and readiness for eternity. Are you spiritually aligned with Christ and God's Word in your life? Those in the eighteenth-century business guild found it important to incorporate Biblical principles in all aspects of their life in order to fully appreciate accomplishments. In holistic medicine, you treat the entire body and not just the symptom, so that the patient is restored to full health. Similarly, the business guild believed that a holistic approach to living uncompromised across their spiritual, personal, and business lives would lead to greater and healthier success.

How should we live our life, and how can we live an uncompromised lifestyle? If we want to be proficient at anything, we are required to study the subject matter, and it is no different with living Godly and Biblically. Many people may attend Church, and it makes us feel good about ourselves, but it does not even begin to expose the vast knowledge that God has for us in His Word. Rule 7 is the starting point for living well in a life of faith.

Rule 7: WHAT IS REQUIRED
Living well is to live according to God's teachings, not compromising on your spiritual integrity. This requires you to be knowledgeable of God's Word.

Therefore, you should utilize your education and study the scriptures to understand what God requires of you. Even if you lack education, you should still seek to learn what God requires of you.

"Continue to think about what is good and worthy of praise. Think about what is true and honorable and right and pure and beautiful and respected." Philippians 4:8 (ERV)

Our spiritual journey must include more than just going to Church on Sunday mornings and maybe joining some fellowship activities. Many years ago, my wife was challenged one day by a person stating that the word "trinity" is not found in the Bible and it confounded her. She related this experience to me, and I really could not dispute the statement either. Over time this question and other questions finally led me to seek answers. Understanding and studying God's Word is crucial and joining a Bible Study may help provide you with deeper learning. Bible Study groups may also become a support group for you as well. If you were asked what you believe about God and the Bible, could you answer easily and thoroughly? This book is not a Bible study, but I do highly recommend educating yourself about the Bible as there is a tremendous wealth of knowledge for personal and workplace life. As a result, God's Word and wisdom is referenced in every chapter and is an important part of being a Godly manager.

Rule 4: LIFE IS SHORT
Life in this world is short and uncertain, filled with emotions of love and joy but also of fear and doubt. However, a wise individual does not dwell on this world as their ultimate life but looks beyond it.

"If only they were wise, if only this was clear to them, and they would give thought to their future!" Deuteronomy 32:29 (BBE)

"Teach us how short our life is, so that we may become wise." Psalms 90:12 (GNT)

Therefore, they make it their business to prepare for the eternal life to come, and doing so in their personal life, their spiritual life, as well as their business life. This is true wisdom!

Studying the Bible brings about intellectual knowledge, but it does not satisfy our emotional and spiritual needs. We may not even understand or know that we are lacking spiritual fulfillment. Rule #4 brings a bit of reality to the forefront of our thoughts, and while it mentions the brevity of life, the focus is on the spiritual quality of your life now! How does one prepare for the eternal life? It starts with having a deep relationship with Christ our Lord daily. It is this full commitment of our mind, body, and soul to God that brings about the greater understanding of life and true wisdom.

Rule 5: LIVE WELL
Death is the ending for this life and the beginning for the eternal life for those who strive to live their life for the Lord and enjoy eternal happiness rather than despair.

"You know very well that the day when the Lord comes again will be a surprise, like a thief who comes at night." 1 Thessalonians 5:2 (ERV)

Rule 6: PREPARE NOW
It is important to live a godly life because death may come unexpectedly and leave no opportunity for "death-bed salvation." If you do not live a godly life, then your death-bed profession might not be from your heart in faith and truthfulness. It may sound like you are trying to insure against all potentialities.

The Bible does talk about the brevity of our earthly existence and whether we are living a life for God. You can see in rules #5 and #6 the result of living your life for God is that you can look forward to an eternal life of happiness rather than despair.

Accepting Christ as your Lord and Savior is not a "Get Out of Jail Free" card, whereby all you have to do is play the card before the end of your life. Instead, accepting Christ is a life-changing event so that you live today in an entirely new way. The life-changing event is not limited to only your personal and spiritual life, but all aspects including your business life as well. If you compartmentalize God, then you are not fully "bought in" to believing in Him to make your life fulfilled in every way and every aspect. Benjamin Franklin stated that, "in this world nothing can be said to be certain, except death and taxes." But I believe this statement falls short. While the world believes in death and taxes, as believers we know with certainty that God blesses you and me with eternal life.

Salvation is not based on doing good works or good deeds, as we cannot earn the gift that God freely gives to those who believe in Christ. As a result of our accepting the gift of salvation, we are invited into the relationship that God wants to have with us through Jesus Christ and the Holy Spirit. This relationship should influence us in all aspects of our lives, including how we manage people and our business.

Some may think that a relationship with God means that we are weak and spineless, but nothing could be further from the truth. In fact, Jesus himself displayed courage, strength, and dedication about bringing the new covenant to Israel. He went up against the leaders of the nation and even those of the Roman empire by giving His own mortal life as a part of the covenant. Obviously, Jesus won the battle in His resurrection, but in doing so He exemplified courage and strength that any of us would be proud of. Being a Christian does not call us to be weak and spineless but gives us strength to follow God and leverage His wisdom in our lives and in our businesses.

CALLED TO MANAGE

We must take God with us beyond our day of worship and into our business week! If you do not have God primarily embedded in your business activities, you are missing opportunities that God has for you. John writes about the Church in Laodicea in the book of Revelation and how they are "*neither hot nor cold*" (Revelations 3:15-16). Similarly, worshipping God on the weekends and forgetting God during the workweek is the same type of failing.

Develop a strong relationship with God and maintain it throughout the entire week. Keeping your relationship with God strong during the work week must be a conscious effort. Therefore, be strong and follow through. It is through your relationship with God that His direction and wisdom is revealed, including guidance on business decisions and relationships. God wants to bring you success, but it may differ from the world's idea of success.

Are you seen as a Godly person and a Godly manager all week long? Are you seen as a person of integrity in all aspects of your life? Who is guiding your decisions, God or the world?

Chapter 2:
What Does Your Name Stand For

One of the most introspective questions that can be asked is, "Who am I?" You already know my thoughts on spirituality, so now we are going to look at other qualities that make up who we are. When you look in the mirror and consider the personality and character of the person there, are you satisfied with what you see?

Most of us will create a mental image of ourselves, the way we would like to be, the way we would want others to see us, and the way we want to be remembered. How is that working out for you? Are you becoming who you imagined yourself to be? It may be time for a reality check. Understanding how others perceive you is the real test of your character. When you walk into your home after work, what does your family think of you? Are you a workaholic, and as a result you are too exhausted to spend quality time with your family? When you walk in the door at work, what do your direct reports and coworkers think of you? Do you have strong relationships with them, are you approachable? What do your direct reports call you behind your back? Are their thoughts of you good or bad? The next three rules help us examine and refine our true character.

Rule 10: FIRM SET OF BELIEFS

Establish a firm set of beliefs, otherwise you may be inconsistent in word and action causing others to question you. This includes, not compromising your beliefs for personal gain or to benefit others. In doing this, you will find confidence in yourself, you will find approval from others, and approval from God. Do not listen to those who are reckless or corrupt.

Have you attended management seminars where you determined your top values, and then sought to understand how they shaped you and your management style? The question for you is, did anyone challenge your values? Are your top values really your top values? Have you genuinely researched your values and beliefs so that you know what drives you or what is most important to you?

In one of these exercises my top five values in order were, Spirituality, Family, Integrity, Relationships, and Service. Then the unthinkable happened, the facilitator challenged my values and I became defensive. How could the facilitator dispute my own "top values?" We should certainly know which values are our most important. After calming down I began to consider his questions, and they were tough. I reanalyzed my actions and behaviors, and most were aligned with my values. However, another value popped up unexpectedly into my top five – Security. While Security would not be my number one value, it would have made it to fourth or fifth on my list. Like the adage that you spend more money on those things most important, you should examine your values regarding the time and money you spend on them.

Can you look back on your life and see those defining moments that shaped who you are? Your values are likely shaped by the defining moments and experiences throughout your life and reviewing those events may provide insight into how they impacted your values. When questioning my own values, I looked back on a time when I was a self-absorbed thirteen-year-old. My father struggled to find work and it led to a mental breakdown whereby he entered a Veterans Affairs Hospital for the next two years. My mother worked in a low-wage job and struggle to keep the household afloat for my sister and me. The first thing she did was negotiate interest-only payments on our home and our car. When things got tougher, she obtained food-stamps so that we would have food on the table. Two major realizations came about from this experience. First was that my mother was stronger than I could understand at the time. Second, and the one that impacts me to this day, I never wanted myself or my family to ever experience anything like that. This is what drives me to be a workaholic because I believe I must ensure that my family is taken care of – providing <u>security</u>. Because I know the power "Security" can have on my life, I can choose not to let it control me. By better understanding the values that drive our behavior, we can better manage our thoughts and actions.

CALLED TO MANAGE

Our values and beliefs shape who we are and what we do, so it is important to understand them. Take some time to determine your values and beliefs.

1. Choose your top values, initially keeping your choices to ten or less.

2. Now the hard part is to narrow the list down to your critical five values. The five that are fundamental to your beliefs.

CALLED TO MANAGE

This is a small list of values. There are hundreds of others you might choose from.

Achievement	Faith	Passion
Advancement	Family	Peace
Adventure	Freedom	Power
Arts	Fun-Pleasure	Prestige
Authority	Growth	Quality
Belonging	Happiness	Recognition
Caring	Health	Relationships
Change	Honesty	Reputation
Challenge	Humor	Respect
Communication	Independence	Responsibility
Compassion	Influence	Security
Competition	Integrity	Self-Realization
Creativity	Justice	Service
Curiosity	Knowledge	Spirituality
Decisiveness	Leadership	Strength
Diversity	Leisure	Success
Effectiveness	Love	Teamwork
Equality	Loyalty	Time
Experience	Meaningful	Trustworthiness
Excellence	Work	Truth
Fairness	Nature	Wisdom

So, what do you spend your time on? If you said Family, do you spend enough time with them? If you said Spirituality, do you spend time with God during your work week, or only on your day of worship?

What influences your decision making? Do your top values come into play with your decision making? Question your choices and understand if there are other values that have a major impact in your life. Just as I discovered my own subconscious connection to the value of Security, is there another value that is influencing your life. Understanding what drives and motivates you will be helpful in making better decisions in your life.

Values and beliefs are important to who we are, but they should not lead us to consider ourselves more important than others. The next rule offers insight into the harmful effects of pride in the workplace.

Rule 9: BLINDED BY PRIDE

"In the same way your light must shine before people, so that they will see the good things you do and praise your Father in heaven." Matthew 5:16 (GNT)

Do not be vain or full of yourself.

"O Lord, to you alone, and not to us, must glory be given because of your constant love and faithfulness." Psalms 115:1 (GNT)

"Who do you think you are? Everything you have was given to you. So, if everything you have was given to you, why do you act as if you got it all by your own power?" 1 Corinthians 4:7 (ERV)

It feels great to have the admiration of others, and it is human to want this for ourselves. However, you will find that pride and vanity are empty of value, many may resent you for it, and God detests it.

CALLED TO MANAGE

It is natural for us to believe that most everyone else will believe the way we do and consider the same things as priorities in their lives. This is the negative aspect of pride, the selfish side which pushes others away. To be prideful and arrogant is to close yourself off from others and therefore to potential ideas, solutions, and strategies. Extreme versions of pride and arrogance are seen on the world stage as dictators and tyrants because they rule according to their own beliefs.

A manager that is filled with selfish pride may display behaviors like those of dictators and tyrants. They will drive their own agenda using the power they wield in order to control the progress and outcome. It becomes a single point of failure because it disallows input, ideas, and solutions from those closest to the effort, when often they are the most knowledgeable. If you value Power, Prestige, and/or Authority, then you might be challenged in keeping your pride and ego in check. Pride is about yourself and less about others, and humility is the opposite of pride.

How can we become humble? Ask God for help and then practice humility until we are comfortable, and it becomes a part of us. For example, our ego wants us to brag about our contributions so we can constantly feed that ego with accolades. Bragging is self-serving and it generates a less than positive perception about you. Consider contributing to the team's effort without having to be recognized. Jesus did not take credit but gave credit to the Father. Instead of receiving the attention for the success of your team, raise them up and praise them to others and to your management. I believe a manager should serve their team following Jesus' example of serving others. As a result, we should place more importance on our direct reports rather than on ourselves, putting our team first. When you make a mistake do you own up to it and apologize? While it is very difficult to do, it can have a strong impact on your direct reports and team.

A leader who has humility will be more valued by the team because of the support they receive from him or her. Your support of the team will continually develop and nurture a collaborative atmosphere so that the best possible work can be done. A humble leader is open to the knowledge and experience of the entire team and therefore increases the likelihood for success. And the team will be more committed to a leader that supports them in their success.

Who am I? Our character is also defined by the actions we carry out.

Rule 34: DO NOT CONFORM TO THE WORLD
Within reason, be willing to live by the rules, laws, and customs of your society and workplace, associating with those who do likewise. Ensure that you maintain your interpersonal and spiritual character, and do not lose yourself to the crowd mentality which often leads to poor character or poor moral decisions.

"Always be ready to defend your confidence [in God] when anyone asks you to explain it. However, make your defense with gentleness and respect." 1 Peter 3:15b (GW)

Do not represent yourself to be holier than others so that you are not branded a fraud. Be careful on entering arguments on controversial points of religion without sufficient knowledge on the subject so that you do not accept distorted Truth. These debates may cause more harm than good.

A reputation is hard to build up and easy to lose. How you live your personal life and your business life is a reflection of your character. Would the way you live your life provide the evidence of a strong moral character, or something less than what you hoped for? Do you "walk the walk" or just "talk the talk?" Does your work life behavior imply that you are a person of integrity, and does it align with your spiritual life?

Another aspect to consider is what impact do you have on future generations. Not only the impact on your descendants and extended family, but also those with whom you worked. When you leave this life how will you be remembered? Will you be remembered and held in high regard for the blessings and contributions you made to your family, friends and business associates? Will you leave a legacy that will continue to benefit others long after you're gone, and will that legacy continue for many generations to come?

What is a good name worth? What are you known for? What do others say about you? What do your direct reports say about you?

> *"If you have to choose between a good reputation and great wealth, choose a good reputation."*
> Proverbs 22:1 (GNT)

CALLED TO MANAGE

Chapter 3:
What Is Your Purpose

What is your purpose? This is a statement which, depending on your circumstances, may be overwhelming or may be completely unknown to you. Your purpose, or vision, is a high-level definition on what you want to accomplish. What do you want your life to mean? You may consider this from an overall standpoint or from different aspects; what do you want your life to mean spiritually, personally, and professionally?

Rule 1: PURPOSE
 A fundamental rule for living a respected and honorable life. Set for yourself a purpose, a goal to work towards in all aspects of your life, a purpose that is reputable and good.

If you have no purpose or goal to guide you, if you are aimlessly working, you will not find fulfilment. An unlawful or immoral purpose will lead to a feeling of guilt, a disrespect from others, and a disrespect for yourself.

CALLED TO MANAGE

We have grown up learning about the separation of Church and state, and we may assume that it applies to separating our spiritual life from our professional life. Companies may state that there should be a separation of "Church" and management. As a believer, our spirituality is in every part of our very being! We cannot separate our faith from the other aspects of our life, including our professional life. Your belief in God will influence your entire life and the deeper your belief the stronger the influence.

God is engaged in our lives and He guides and directs us if we listen and obey. Have you received a revelation whereby God has called you to manage people? Are you a manager, and is that exactly where God wants you to be? I believe God calls me to manage and lead people! Now God has placed on my heart a responsibility to write this book on people management from a Godly perspective. I am compelled to write it and even while doing so I come to realize that it does not matter if this book ever gets published. And even if no one reads it except my family, it has made me evaluate and reflect on my purpose and experiences, what I have learned, and the scriptures which encourage me to live life out the best I can. God has a purpose for every one of His children and He desires that we accept His purpose for our lives. Our commitment is to obey the calling God has placed upon our heart.

> *"It was he who "gave gifts to people"; he appointed some to be apostles, others to be prophets, others to be evangelists, others to be pastors and teachers."*
> Ephesians 4:11 (GNT)

CALLED TO MANAGE

What is your professional purpose? Is your calling aligned to the management and leadership of people? A Godly manager is called to be a servant to their direct reports. You should desire to support them so that they might find greater success and achievement in their careers. Knowing your purpose and being able to easily articulate that to others provides structure. It is your high-level outline which will help you from aimlessly drifting off the path to your purpose.

Have you ever been uncertain about your path or choices in life? I initially dropped out of college after a single semester because I was unprepared, especially for majoring in engineering. I restarted college multiple times considering a major in accounting and then electronics. Obviously, I did not know my purpose and I bounced around aimlessly. I look back over my life now and it was there in front of me the entire time: managing people. I started managing a convenience store when I was nineteen years old. I had several years of management experience when it finally clicked, and I went back to college and worked towards my degree in business. Are you struggling to find direction in your life? Are you wandering aimlessly?

What is your Purpose? What is God's will for your life? If you already know the answer then you are ahead of many others. However, if you are uncertain about your purpose in life or in your profession then you need to work through the issue and find the answer. It may not be your ultimate purpose but taking a first step or potentially testing the possibilities can help point you in the right direction. In the last chapter, we talked about where we spend our time and determining those top activities that may have greater value or influence on our lives. Consider this aspect regarding your purpose or goals to find what you enjoy doing in your professional life. You have likely worked on and completed projects in your work life, but were you equally successful on all projects? What about projects that you had a passion for, were you more successful and fulfilled? What is your passion in your professional life? What is your vision of yourself in the future?

You may not know what your ultimate purpose is initially, but you can still work towards a specific goal or milestone that you believe aligns with what you envision your purpose might be. As you accomplish each step, goal, or milestone; take time to reflect if your accomplishment aligns with your potential purpose.

How do you feel about the work you have been doing? Do you believe you are moving in the right direction towards your purpose? From the rule above, did you find the work "reputable and good," or "fulfilling?" If you do not find any fulfillment in your accomplishments then your reflection should include the possibility of making a course correction or even turning toward a completely new direction. While this may sound like a setback or even failure, please realize that it is progress. Learning what brings fulfillment and satisfaction may require learning what does not. Progress includes elimination of activities that do not accomplish or meet your end goals. Eliminating possibilities will reduce your choices and help you find your ultimate solution faster than if you had not taken those steps at all.

CALLED TO MANAGE

Be careful and do not let obstacles and challenges dissuade you from believing in and pursuing your purpose. During my late twenties, I managed a new car dealership service department. There, I inherited a situation in which the head mechanic controlled the payroll for all the mechanics, thus ensuring their allegiance. When trying to assert any influence over the mechanics, the head mechanic would exert his control over the team. He thereby maintained control and power over the team of mechanics. Tensions continued to heat up within the service department to a point whereby the dealership owner called me into his office. The owner, business manager, comptroller and I met to discuss the situation. The owner arrived at a decision. He told me to go back to the service department and run the business myself, or else he would fire everyone and start all over. I went back to the service department and met with the head mechanic, explaining that I would be controlling all payroll and management going forward. This resulted in the head mechanic and the best mechanic resigning to open their own repair shop. A couple of mechanics whose performance was inadequate were also terminated. It took a year before the several remaining mechanics finally began to understand that they were free of domination. The atmosphere in the service department was more open for mechanics to take initiative and increase productivity and, as a result, to be compensated and rewarded for it. This was also when the service department began to turn around our quality ratings to become the best in the sales region. You may have to persevere through a lot of stress and uncertainty, but ultimately you can overcome the obstacles and challenges and stay dedicated to your purpose.

With regards to your professional purpose and goals, you should consider sharing your "vision" with the team. If the team believes in your purpose then they might align their work and efforts to help you accomplish your purpose, especially if they see it as mutually beneficial. Even though we want our direct reports to align their work and efforts with our purpose, we must not force our purpose to be theirs. Everyone should have their own purpose in life. However, you must also be prepared to learn, or maybe even actively try to determine, if there are purposes and goals within your team that are aligned against your own. If some of the team is not aligned with you then they will not be working in the direction you want to go. Within your team you may have someone that is seen as a leader. It could be someone with seniority or maybe charisma. These other leaders can help lead the team toward the vision you have set out for them, or they can lead them astray. Teams that are divided in their purpose can generate frustrations leading to disruption or even dissention. It is critical that as leaders we build a vision and purpose for the team so that everyone can align their work and efforts with our mission and goals. The team must trust you as their leader so that they will support you and potentially support your vision. Also, realize that differing visions may also come from your fellow managers, your boss, or from the company overall. If your vision differs with your boss' or the company's, then you may need to review the situation carefully to determine how you might move forward. For example, can you pursue your goals in parallel with pursuing the company goals? Then you may need to develop distinct plans for each goal. Other purposes in your life should not conflict with one another. However, if your professional purpose contradicts your spiritual beliefs then you need to review the situation closely.

Have you found your purpose in managing and leading people? Have you worked towards success in your purpose? My efforts toward fulfilling my professional purpose included "on the job" training, but to refine my knowledge I went back to college to complete my degree. Have you discovered other calls or purposes in the other aspects of your life that may be of a personal or a spiritual nature? Other callings in my life would include organizing and leading several mission trips for fifteen to twenty-five people. After you have **identified your purpose**, you need to **create your plan** and **take action**. Continue reading to learn more about planning and taking action.

We often see successful people retire from their original job and pursue a second career. This could mean that your purpose has been fulfilled and then you find a new purpose for your life. It may also mean that your purpose has moved into another area of focus or calling. For example, many people will continue to serve but in a spiritual or philanthropic manner.

CALLED TO MANAGE

Is God calling you to do something new for your next career?

> *"I know the plans that I have for you, declares the LORD. They are plans for peace and not disaster, plans to give you a future filled with hope."*
> Jeremiah 29:11 (GW)

PART 2: Your Plan

CALLED TO MANAGE

Chapter 4:
Accountable to Yourself

There are situations and people in our lives that will continually challenge our beliefs, our values, and who we are. So how do we maintain accountability to ourselves through these challenges? Sometimes the dilemma we face may be coming from within ourselves. My first challenge, or temptation, in the business environment occurred when I was fourteen years old working in a small auto repair shop. Regularly I would become thirsty and crave a soft drink. A few times when I did not have the money for the drink machine, I would take what I needed from a tray on the owners' desk where they kept their extra change. The couple that owned the repair shop confronted me for taking money and I confessed. I was ashamed and afraid, but this amazing couple addressed my behavior in a gentle yet firm manner. We discussed a plan for reimbursement and a solution going forward. This was a "learning moment" about the value of honesty and integrity. This business-couple cared about their employees. They shaped me into a better human being for which I am forever grateful. We should hope to support our directs like this couple demonstrated with theirs.

Rule 20: AVOID TEMPTATION

Turn and run from temptation to do wrong. Surround yourself with honorable and virtuous people, books, and content. If you must face temptation, call on God to give you strength and determination to resist. Be always prepared so that you are not attacked when your defenses are weak or unprepared.

"Keep watch and pray that you will not fall into temptation. The spirit is willing, but the flesh is weak."
Matthew 26:41 (GNT)

It is easier not to play with fire so that you are not burned. If you are not sure you can win against temptation, you should not engage.

Have you ever had a crisis of conscience where you could "win" the deal, but it would hurt the other party? Early in my career I managed an electronics retail store and my compensation was based on salary plus commission. A family entered my store and I noticed that they had an older dilapidated car and their clothes were clean but worn. The young father wanted to buy a new stereo and that is when I found myself in a quandary, a crisis of conscience. My head was telling me to sell them a high-end unit, but my heart was saying that I should show them something within their budget. At some point we hit that tipping point between our own selfish desires for success and the high road of integrity. Integrity won out that day!

Sales may or may not be your strong point, but it is a critical aspect of every business in order to survive. For some of us there is also the service side of the business where we might thrive. We should all hope our companies have great salespeople. It is these great salespeople who bring in lots of business so that the entire company and all its employees can benefit.

Throughout our lives we grow and develop, including our personalities and our character. Every life experience will shape us whether it is a mind-blowing change or a confirmation of something we already believe in. We should especially learn from those moments that bring about a crisis of conscience because it is in these moments where we might experience tremendous growth.

What are your rules for living with integrity and good character? As a manager I based mine on three simple commitments. I will give you trust and respect unless you do not act with integrity. I will work to earn your trust and respect. I expect that each of us will trust and respect the company and its mission and values.

Rule 21: LAZINESS LEADS TO TEMPTATION
Stay focused on your task and work diligently, avoiding distraction and laziness. Too much time on one's hands may lead to doing something we should not do or giving in to temptation. Therefore, we should fill our excess time with our work and business so that we are not tempted with sinful activities. Laziness, or the sin of slothfulness, may consume us unless we remember that God is with us and provides opportunities to do His work in the world. Many people claim to be Christian but make no effort to exemplify Godliness in this world.

CALLED TO MANAGE

Have you ever been surprised when you consider the root cause of a sin or poor business decision? The Bible passage about King David and Bathsheba (2 Samuel 11:1-18) leads most people to associate David with the sins of lust and adultery. Some think of the sin of murder since David sent Bathsheba's husband to his death. Consider the root cause that started this chain-reaction of events where King David spiraled deeper and deeper into trouble. David's initial sin was slothfulness or laziness. As the king, David should have led his troops in battle, but he chose to stay home. As king he did not need to work, so he had a lot of time on his hands. This is when people are often pulled into trouble because temptation becomes more abundant and inviting when we do not have a task or activity to fill our time.

Our world today provides us with numerous conveniences, access to knowledge and information, and everything you can imagine exists digitally on the Internet. It also offers us a multitude of distractions that in themselves have the power to either enrich or corrupt us. We live in a time of enlightenment and knowledge, a true information age greater than ever before in history. However, the content that we have at our fingertips is not always decent and healthy.

People often relate to their body as a temple. They voice concerns that the body's health is based on what we put into it. For example, utilizing drugs inappropriately has a harmful effect, or poor food choices will also harm the body. Similarly, consider what is put into your mind and the impact it has on your health. We hear stories of kids or young people being desensitized to violence to the point that there is no respect for the lives of others. We are influenced by the content we consume through a number of mediums including television programs, movies, books, the Internet and more. What are you putting into your mind, and how is that shaping your thoughts and beliefs? Do you tend to lean towards aspects of laziness with too much downtime, or find activities that enrich? Have you considered the activities associated with your downtime, do they build you up, or tear you down?

You decide how your time is spent. Is it enriching or destructive? Do you struggle with laziness or in making poor choices? You are not alone. God knows the human condition; He knows you and me and that we will at times fall on our face. It does not matter how advanced our world is or will become, because He anticipates our shortcomings. God provides us with the Holy Spirit who is with us always. That spirit of God in us guides and directs us if we are willing to listen.

Rule 8: FROM WHERE DOES STRENGTH COME
Pray to God for the strength to accomplish His calling for your life and that nothing will deter you or tempt you to sin, not anyone or anything.

Wisdom helps to determine a course of action. The Holy Spirit provides guidance. God imparts strength for taking action. Without God's strength your efforts will fade, so ask God to instill renewed strength each morning and throughout the day.

CALLED TO MANAGE

"Don't be afraid of those who kill the body but cannot kill the soul. Instead, fear the one who can destroy both body and soul in hell." Matthew 10:28 (GW)

"If people are ashamed of me and what I say in this unfaithful and sinful generation, the Son of Man will be ashamed of those people when he comes with the holy angels in his Father's glory." Mark 8:38 (GW)

"I will keep my solemn promise to obey your just instructions." Psalms 119:106 (GNT)

"We must obey God, not men." Acts 5:29b (GNT)

When I was thirty years old I was driving by my parents' house and saw an ambulance parked out front of it. My first thought was, "They cannot be here at **MY** house." But the front door was open, and my second thought was, "That's not good." So, I parked and ran up to meet the paramedics coming out the front door with my dad on a stretcher. I was told that he was hooked up to oxygen and an EKG machine because he was having chest pains. Still not good, but the first responders got there on time! They put him in the ambulance, and I stood there watching through the open doors. Then my dad went into cardiac arrest. There was no backboard underneath him, so the paramedic raised his fist up high and pounded down on my dad's chest again and again. They revived him and I was thinking, "It will be okay, he will just get a bypass or something." They told me which hospital they were taking him to so I could meet them there. I closed and locked up the house before heading to the hospital.

That was the last time I saw my dad alive. The memories are still vivid of the paramedic pounding on my dad's chest. It is still etched into my brain and it is like tunnel-vision because I do not remember seeing or noticing anyone around me. I felt alone and that is still how I remember it over 30 years later.

It is extraordinarily difficult to effectively handle the major stresses of life alone, especially without God, without Christ, without the Church, and without Christian brothers and sisters. This is especially true for stressful events in life such as the death of a loved one. Here is the rest of the story: The next vivid memory I have about my father's passing was of lots of food being brought into my parents' home. My adult brother and sister wondered who all these people were that brought us so much food? With my emotions reaching a breaking point, I exclaimed that "This is my *Church* family!" At that moment some understanding started to seep into my thoughts. The next memory was of the funeral a couple of days later, and it was amazing to me how many people attended my dad's funeral! They did not all know my dad but many of them were there for me! I never previously thought much about what it meant to attend a funeral for others, but when my friends and Church family did it for me, I got it. The realization came to me that we are not alone, our friends and family are there for us. More importantly, God is there showing His great love for us through the "body of Christ," through the "body of believers."

CALLED TO MANAGE

This story may sound out of place here in the context of this chapter, but it is not. When evaluating where our strength comes from, we must all remember, or learn, that we are never alone. God is with us through the Holy Spirit, and He is with us through our Christian brothers and sisters. It is important to have a support structure to help you when you are feeling down or angry, or to share the joy you are feeling. Everyone needs a support structure, and I would recommend a Christian support structure. Rule #8 reminds us that God is always there for us to lean on. Prayer is a principal means of building your relationship with God, along with worship, study and praise.

When we look at the business environment today it seems that everyone is expected to drive their career toward success at all costs. They should climb and conquer the mountain even if it means stepping on the backs of others to get there. However, we should take a step back while on the mountain and consider the satisfaction received for a job well done, and therefore consider the "how" regarding our path to success. There is nothing wrong with success, as there is nothing wrong with money. However, if we crave success or money and will do anything to get it, then our achievement lacks integrity and we may find ourselves alone.

Chapter 5:
Accountable in Your Relationships

How are we perceived? This is a question we should ask ourselves so that we can better understand how it might impact our interactions, conversations, and relationships with others. Our words and our behaviors will impact how others engage with us, and it can enhance or diminish the value received from that engagement.

We have all been placed into uncomfortable situations at some point in our lives, and the anxiety levels rise within us. Our "need" to engage in these circumstances brings risk, jeopardizing our security and comfort level further still. Often it is our own misplaced fear that will control us and lead us to make poor decisions.

An example may be a business negotiation or a major purchase, beginning with cordial greetings and "get to know you" questions. This conversational exchange typically begins with very safe topics. After reaching an initial level of comfort, the discussion gets deeper and more engaging. We reach a point where we feel uncomfortable, and often we will begin to employ defense mechanisms. It may even become combative whereby we feel the other person is going for our jugular. Fight, flight, or freeze may be the next defense mechanism to emerge, but in any circumstance the conversation has long stopped being productive.

Rule 14: SPEAK WELL OF OTHERS
If you keep your conversation friendly and pleasant you will maintain a good rapport with those whom you converse. Additionally, you should always strive to listen as well as engage in pleasant and friendly conversation.

Avoid communications or speech that includes sarcasm or the ridicule of others, for the recipient may not see it as humorous but will remember the insult.

We can probably recall situations like the scenario above, or a negotiation or interview that did not go so well. In these situations, we likely felt threatened. We all want to feel like we are accepted by our peers, our teammates, and our organization. With acceptance, there is a feeling of belonging where everyone can trust and depend on one another, and it provides a level of safety and security. It provides a place where we feel free to try new things, specifically free from fear. It is fear that keeps us from taking risks, whether it be with our job, our investments, or negotiations.

The question you must ask yourself is, are you the person that makes conversation easily and extends grace, or are you the person that must always end up on top? Do you have to win even if it means going for the other person's jugular? While you may not be that person that goes for the jugular, does your pride drive you to be on top? Fear often drives the other person in this scenario to flee or to be quiet and not speak up. Fear will stilt a person's willingness to share and there can be a loss of valuable input and knowledge.

When the conversation is more adversarial, are we cultivating an atmosphere of fear? If fear is present among those in the conversation, will we really learn as much? However, if we offered grace in our conversations, would those participating tend to open up faster? If they take some risk and still feel safe and secure due to our graciousness, could we go even deeper and deeper? We should strive to make the other party feel welcome, appreciated and important, and as a result continue building their self-worth and trust. Listening is not easy for many people; we are too busy wanting to put forth our own thoughts and opinions. You have likely heard it said that God intended us to listen more because He gave us two ears and a single mouth, therefore we should listen twice as much as we talk.

> *"Good people will be remembered as a blessing...A good person's words are a fountain of life."* Proverbs 10:7a & 11a (GNT)

Are we seen as a person providing encouragement to those who know us? Do others see us as a blessing that God has placed in their lives? Do we provide a healthy and nourishing environment that is safe and secure for our family, friends and coworkers?

Have you ever been confronted by a decision that causes you to hesitate? We have all had to deal with those decisions, but sometimes there are decisions that might even paralyze us for a time. If you overcame the paralysis and made a decision, how did that occur? Did you "tough it out" and just move forward on your own, or did you have supportive family members or friends who provided encouragement or wise counsel? You have likely benefited immensely because of people who have supported you in your personal life, professional life, and hopefully in your spiritual life! We must be that supporting person to instill encouragement and offer counsel to others. We are to build up and support others so that they will receive God's blessings in their lives, and in the ***decisions*** they are making. Some wisdom I learned is to never make a decision until you have to; time may reveal another option or additional information to make a better decision.

However, we must understand that before others will accept our advice and support, they must trust us. The measure to which they will consider and utilize our input will correspond to the degree of trust they have in us.

Rule 12: LIFE OF INTEGRITY
Be that man of high integrity so that others may see and respect you for these traits and your "word" will carry influence. If you talk about integrity but do not live it, then others will find out and you will be considered unreliable.

CALLED TO MANAGE

"If you make a promise to God, keep your promise. Don't be slow to do what you promised. God is not happy with fools. Give God what you promised to give him." Ecclesiastes 5:4 (ERV)

This rule brings me back to the old idiom, "if you're going to talk the talk, you've got to walk the walk." It is also related to the "talk is cheap" axiom whereby a person expounds information or advice of seeming importance yet does not even follow it themselves.

Have you ever felt like the world we live in today has diminished the importance of accountability and dependability, and that it is okay to cut corners or not fulfill your responsibilities? A friend of mine whom I will call Joe had a situation that exemplifies this well:

A strong springtime storm damaged the wooden privacy fence between Joe's house and his neighbor's, and to Joe's surprise their neighbor came to their door to see about sharing the costs to repair the fence. Joe agreed to get an estimate, and then shared it with the neighbor. After the neighbor agreed to the cost, Joe had the fence repaired and presented the bill to the neighbor who then began to make excuses and avoid him. In an effort to make it easier, Joe offered his neighbor a payment plan, but still nothing. A year went by, Joe saw his neighbor outside and decided to talk with him. The neighbor would not make eye contact, but Joe patiently waited. When he finally acknowledged Joe, the neighbor then denied agreeing to the repair even though Joe has a text message confirming the agreement. He told Joe to take him to small claims court.

Situations like this produce an environment of mistrust and deceit in any relationship. The lack of accountability and dependability in our society today hampers personal connections in our social circles and in larger environments such as the neighborhood and community. Society seems to be evolving more into a self-centered state and it seems that "good faith" and integrity are not as important. It is appealing and even tempting to get pulled into the same desires of self-centeredness and self-indulgence, and it is easier not to worry about anyone but yourself. However, this selfish environment is not limited to yourself, but it impacts those around you! It will continue to spiral into the depths of darkness including mistrust, deceit, cheating, and theft. Compare this selfish world to the seven deadly sins and we realize that they are deeply embedded in the culture today (Lust, Gluttony, Greed, Slothfulness, Wrath, Envy, and Pride).

However, God calls us to be of high integrity and to extend respect to others even though it will be more difficult than conforming with the world's view.

Do you "walk the walk," or are you all talk and no substance? Do others trust you so that you can have open, honest and valuable interactions?

We must try to "walk the walk" all the time, but no one is perfect by any means. Even if you have earned the trust of your peers and direct reports through your actions, it is not a one-time deal. It is an ongoing effort so that we do not lose the trust of our friends and acquaintances and those you will come to know in the future. When you garner the trust of others, you will find that the conversations and engagements with them are of greater value. God has called us to live a life of integrity, not just for Him, but for ourselves and all people with whom we come into contact.

CALLED TO MANAGE

Chapter 6:
Accountable in Managing Others

As a manager, or if you want to become a manager, you should have a desire to help others to be the best that they can be. God's Word states, *"Whatever you do, work at it with all your heart, as though you were working for the Lord,"* Colossians 3:23 (GNT). Therefore, we are called to develop and grow our directs toward their success. Helping others succeed in any aspect of their life can be a blessing for you.

Managing people is a tremendous responsibility because we hold the livelihood of our direct reports and their families in our control. Managers must care about their direct reports, helping them to be successful and fulfilled in all aspects of their lives. When we are assigned a new direct report or a new team, how do we get started? Of course, we want to establish a relationship and get to know them better. Before we can provide guidance and set expectations we must develop an initial relationship with them. In some business cultures there are certain customs or rituals leading to relationship development.

CALLED TO MANAGE

Several years ago, I traveled with a Church group deep into Mexico to work with an orphanage for teenage boys. When the boys neared adolescence, they moved out of the main orphanage to separate them from the girls. The missionary pastor was about to relocate the boys to a small farm outside of town and needed to purchase a few goats from local farmers. We traveled to meet a farmer in a local village and the pastor asked us to wait while he negotiated with them. They talked animatedly for five or ten minutes, with each of them lifting their shirt and pointing at their abdomens. We wondered what in the world they were talking about.

After the pastor had made the deal and got the goat, we asked him about the negotiations and what all the pointing meant. He stated that you must get to know each other before you can negotiate. So, when the farmer started talking about a recent surgery, the pastor showed him his own surgical scar. They established a comfort level with one another, a friendly relationship, then they could negotiate the deal.

Similarly, we should follow this same strategy in our role as managers - we continually build a relationship, negotiate, and close the deal. We should start with building a relationship with everyone on the team so that we come to know them well. You may need to be cautious about having close friendships with your direct reports because it may make effective management very difficult. Both parties must understand that managing in the workplace must override your friendship. As we better understand everyone, we can discuss their role and job performance, then discuss

CALLED TO MANAGE

opportunities and set goals. Depending on a person's current level of work, we want to motivate them to either meet expectations of the core job, to excel, or even to stretch for that next level of performance. One common question that a direct report will ask next is about how they can accomplish the goals set for them. The next best step is NOT to tell them how. Instead, coach them through the "How" by asking leading questions so that they come to their own understanding and put plans in place based on their own individuality. They do not have to perform tasks the way we would. By coaching them, asking leading questions, sharing ideas, they will develop their own plan and they will have ownership in the plan because they developed it for themselves. You are teaching them to plan and strategize for themselves and not to be dependent on others. Their likelihood of success will increase and their satisfaction with the work will also be higher. There will always be those direct reports that simply cannot get off the starting blocks. In these situations, we may have to provide precise guidance on how to accomplish their basic job duties and progress forward in their career.

This is an ongoing cyclical journey with each of our direct reports and basically, we should try to apply this methodology each time we have a one-on-one meeting with them. Try to meet with your direct reports at least once per month and preferably every two weeks. Each meeting should build upon the previous one so that your direct report can continually move towards success. We cannot take weeks or months focusing on a single step or aspect with our direct reports. Each meeting should have relationship building, goal setting, and development of an action plan. Each meeting will continue to improve our relationships with our direct reports, and the resulting value will also improve. While the One-on-one Meeting will help guide our direct reports in their jobs, it is not intended to be a deep dive into a person's career development plan. Even after several meetings, we may not fully understand our direct reports, but we do begin to recognize what motivates them. We need to learn not only what motivates them, but also their purpose. They may not know exactly what their purpose is, but we should consider this aspect as we guide our team members in their One-on-one Meetings.

Where do you start with a new direct report or new team? The next rule is on target here. Prioritize the agenda for your next One-on-one Meeting and depending on the criticality of the issues you may want to schedule sooner rather than later. Your initial agenda should include those jobs or tasks that are most important or time sensitive, or even more important if you need to meet to discuss corrective actions with a direct report. We cannot be afraid to tackle the serious issues with our direct reports no matter how uncomfortable it may be.

Rule 11: YOUR WORD REFLECTS YOU
Prioritize your topics of conversation, negotiations, or guidance so that the most important matters are taken care of first.

CALLED TO MANAGE

> *"Instead, be concerned above everything else with the Kingdom of God and with what he requires of you."* Matthew 6:33 (GNT)
>
> After completing the more serious matters, focus next on issues of lesser importance or of charity, carrying out all with a mindset of respect. As a result, you will become known and respected for your professional attention and integrity.
>
> If your level of communication is inappropriate, facetious or frivolous, then the value of your reputation and expertise will be diminished. Furthermore, God will always know your heart and character.

Your direct reports want to know if they "fit" into your world, the environment you have created within your team and organization. This happens when your team gets to know you as a leader and a person, and it is based on your every action and interaction. You and your team spend a lot of time together, building a communal relationship with one another and with you as their leader. They learn from their relationships established within the environment that you helped to create, and from that they can determine who to follow and depend on.

Every environment will have multiple levels of management with various types of managers throughout the organization's hierarchy. As a manager, you have a higher status or job-level than your direct reports which provides you authority over the team.

CALLED TO MANAGE

Authority makes you a manager, but how you engage with your team determines if you are a leader. In most situations, you are not the only leader engaging with your team. There will be leaders from within the team which may be true peer leadership or potential peer pressure, depending on how they influence the rest of the team. You should encourage positive peer leadership among the team. However, if you are not engaged with your team and leading them, their peer-leaders or other leaders may persuade the team to focus their efforts in another direction. Are you engaged with the team, instilling the vision and leading them to success?

Have you ever had a boss who did not trust your judgement? When managing for another new car dealership, I also led their service department from being one of the worst-rated to one of the top-rated dealers in the sales region. One day a car was towed in for a customer who was traveling across the country. They had previously broken down two hundred miles away, but the previous dealership did not correctly resolve the problem. When explaining our diagnosis with the other dealership they agreed to reimburse us for the costs of repair. We repaired the car and I let the customer leave to continue their journey. The cashier was upset and stated I could not let the customer leave without paying, whereby I explained that the other dealer would reimburse us. The cashier feared potential consequences from management because of my decision, so the cashier contacted the comptroller. The comptroller also stated that I did not have the authority to allow the other dealer to reimburse us. So, it was a learning experience, but what came next became an even deeper education for me. When I received my monthly commission check a couple of days later, the comptroller had subtracted the repair cost from my check. The reimbursement arrived and I was repaid for the deduction from my check. Here is what I really learned: despite my proven track record, the management did not trust my decision involving a minor repair bill. The lack of trust and support led to my resignation a few weeks later, and management could not understand why I was leaving. They offered a twenty percent raise in salary, but I still turned them down. No one wants to be in an environment of mistrust. You **cannot buy trust!**

Trust is incredibly difficult to earn, and it usually takes a repetition of positive experiences from the person wanting to earn that trust. As difficult as it is to gain that trust, if you lose it, that trust becomes tremendously more difficult to win back again, if at all. Abraham Maslow describes a person's "Hierarchy of Needs" (1943) whereby they seek to have their physiological and psychological needs met. It begins with the physiological needs relating to survival including food, water, shelter and rest. The next most important "needs" are related to feeling safe and secure. In the business workplace, direct reports trust their managers to provide that environment of safety and security. We engage with direct reports by building strong professional relationships with them, and it is through relationships that we build the environment of trust. This environment should embrace the team as a whole and instill safety and security in their workplace. This is important so that they feel they have the freedom to perform at their best, to push the boundaries, and attempt new ideas. The alternative is that the team will continue to do what they have always done because it is safe, and therefore will potentially become obsolete.

Rule 13: TREAT OTHERS WELL
Love your neighbor and extend goodwill toward all, including strangers and enemies. Lean on the Lord who empowers you, and in return you will honor His will. For Christ died for all sinners including you and your enemies. In carrying out this directive, you cannot hold on to anger or ill-will in your heart and honor God at the same time.

"Get rid of all bitterness, passion, and anger. No more shouting or insults, no more hateful feelings of any sort. Instead, be kind and tender-hearted to one another, and forgive one another, as God has forgiven you through Christ." Eph. 4:31-32 (GNT)

Do not hold prejudice against another for being different than yourself.

"As a servant of the Lord, you must not argue. You must be kind to everyone. You must be a good teacher, and you must be patient. You must gently teach those who don't agree with you. Maybe God will let them change their hearts so that they can accept the truth." 2 Timothy 2:24-25 (ERV)

There may be times where you find it necessary to defend yourself, but you should not go beyond what is required for your defense to retaliate or bring damage against another.

"Never take revenge, my friends, but instead let God's anger do it. Do not let evil defeat you; instead, conquer evil with good." Romans 12:19a & 21 (GNT)

If you love your neighbors, then it is difficult to hate them.

Extending goodwill toward strangers and enemies is a challenging task to accomplish in society and is difficult in the workplace. It is frustrating to see managers who disregard or overlook their direct reports and consider them a means to an end. Another situation that is hard to see is managers who are too focused at climbing the corporate ladder and do not care who gets stepped on along the way. However, we cannot allow our frustration or anger drive our own poor response to these situations, but we must give it over to God and trust Him to handle it. Anger takes away our peace and causes our stress levels to spike. We can spread unrest and anger, or we can instill peace and calm into our environment and that of our team.

God calls us to avoid arguments, but we are not required to agree with everyone. When we disagree, we should approach the situation with patience and kindness. Sometimes it feels like "patience and kindness" is too Biblically based and the real world does not operate this way. For example, if we chose not to listen and only force our opinion onto others when there are disagreements, then we will likely find the other party becoming defensive. Defensive posturing wastes time because we still must get back to a position of collaboration and trust for the discussion to move forward in a positive manner. Establishing a relationship of trust will greatly further your progress towards a solution. When we are attacked or disparaged in some way, we are expected to defend our position or character, not by a counterattack, but in the same Biblical manner of kindness and patience. Ultimately, does the other party see us as a Godly role model for progress, or someone who must win at all costs?

The scripture from Rule #13 stated that we should "conquer evil with good," which is like killing them with kindness. While this is a very simple story, it is one I have remembered for many years. When managing a 24-hour convenience store, a particular customer came in every morning. Each day, I greeted him as he entered whereupon he would get a large cup of coffee and write a check for several extra dollars for spending money. I wrote his driver's license number on the check, gave him his cash, and told him to have a good day as he departed. The customer never spoke a word during the entire transaction, and this went on every day for a couple of months. One day the unexpected happened. He came in as usual, got his coffee and wrote his check. I then wrote his driver's license number on the check before he could get his ID out of his wallet. He was shocked and for the first time he asked how I knew his driver's license number. I simply stated that after dozens of checks, I had memorized his driver's license number. He laughed and when I told him to have a good day, he stated the same in return. While we never became real friends, we did have short conversations each morning after. Love those that are difficult, offering kindness without any return expectation, persevering to make a connection.

We talked about extending goodwill to strangers and enemies, but what about our direct reports? We are called to treat our direct reports with patience and kindness so that our relationship with them continues to grow and mature. A strong relationship allows us as managers to have open and honest conversations to help and guide our direct reports in their daily job and career. Building a relationship is not a one-way street; we must be open about ourselves with our direct reports so that they can better understand our position, our background, our goals and our values. Being open with your team is an important aspect of building trust with them, whereby they begin to see a safe place in which to work.

There is one major difference in Christianity as compared to other beliefs, and that is the gift of grace given to all who accept. It is not something we have to earn. It is not about what we do for God, but what God does for us. However, we cannot stop short because the next step should include the scripture from James that proclaims, "*faith without works is dead,*" James 2:17 (BBE). It is because of our faith that we desire to follow God's will and do His work. While our efforts will never be equal to God's, we should consider the model that God sets out for us. As a leader, we should show our direct reports grace and mercy while we also work to earn their trust. The relationship we can build and nurture with our teams will create an environment where direct reports are able to reach their full potential.

However, there will be times when you have direct reports that cannot or will not live up to the potential you need from them. It may be that their desires and purpose has changed, or possibly the person is not the right "fit" for the role they are in. Through our One-on-one Meetings we should have built a relationship and established the expectations for the job. If the person is struggling to perform the job, then our meetings should have gotten increasingly more specific about the minimum requirements and the action plan to accomplish those requirements. If possible, we should explore any possibilities whereby we could place the direct report into another role for which they might be better suited. For myself, I need to know if there are any other possible alternatives. As we begin to determine that this person cannot meet the core requirements of the job, and there is not an alternate role, we should increase the frequency of the One-on-one Meetings. In these meetings, we must document their levels of performance against the core requirements. When it comes down to delivering a poor performance review, or possibly terminating the individual, there should never be a surprise. If the direct report is surprised, then we have failed at our job. The actual termination meeting should be conducted with the utmost respect, care and consideration. They should be specifically told about the decision to terminate their employment along with the relative facts previously discussed with the direct report throughout their recent One-on-one Meetings. It should be short, because again, there should be no surprises. Sometimes it is a relief for the individual, and an opportunity to find another job that better suits them. A new job that makes them happier will likely improve their overall happiness in life. If they are unhappy or stressed in their current job, then they are likely unhappy and stressed in their life in general.

This book does not intend to provide a "cookie-cutter" approach to managing people, because there is tremendous value in the diversity of people and the diversity of experiences. Everyone can contribute to the assistance of others using the different talents God has given us. Together we have greater value because we all bring different strengths, capabilities, knowledge and wisdom.

Every employee should expect to have great people managers to guide and counsel them throughout their careers! I sincerely hope that this book will encourage current and aspiring people managers to seek to be the best they can be for their teams. And more importantly, I pray that God will provide you the wisdom and guidance to be great people managers.

Rule 15: HELP THOSE WHO NEED IT
Based on your ability, give back to help the poor and needy of your community. You will feel contentment and satisfaction, and possibly earn the respect of all those who know you.

The resources you have are entrusted to you by God, so you must be accountable for your use of these resources. If you have considerable disposable resources, yet donate little, then your heavenly reward will reflect your minimal charity.

Giving of your gifts and service above what is expected of you is good for your soul spiritually and emotionally. As stewards of everything God has entrusted us with, we are expected to share these blessings from God with others who may be less fortunate than ourselves.

As a leader and manager, we can use an opportunity for charitable work and combine that with an event for our teams. Having your team work together for charity can be a tremendous teambuilding activity. The team's relationship with one another can reach increased levels of emotional connections because we learn more about each other regarding our compassion and generosity. This can be an emotional high for the team and they may become closer to one another.

While we may not be expected to affect a direct report's emotional and spiritual wellbeing, as leaders we can have a tremendous influence over our teams. As Godly people, we are a role model regardless if we want to be or not. We influence how people perceive God through our daily lives. Our teams see how we live our lives in all aspects including our business and professional abilities, our emotional characteristics, our mental attributes, and our spirituality. Even though some of our team may not believe in God, they will see us as God's representatives. How well is our team seeing God through us?

Chapter 7:
Decisions and Wise Counsel

Have you ever ignored or disregarded someone and later discovered you missed out on the wisdom they tried to share? I worked in a foreign car repair shop during my teenage years. One day while the owner was away the building landlord dropped by. After a few minutes of small talk, the landlord made a suggestion pertaining to the work I was doing. Being an "all knowing" sixteen-year-old, I blew him off. The landlord became a little annoyed with me and he commented, "*Listen to advice, it is free, and **you can choose to use it or not**.*" That exchange has stuck with me for more than forty years.

Truly listening to good advice is a learning opportunity. Even if it does not apply to your life today it may become helpful later. In contrast, rejecting the advice is to live in arrogance and continue in ignorance. At some point in our lives we finally learn to listen to good advice and wise counsel. Then we have to determine if it is the right decision for our circumstances.

In 1 Kings 12, there is the story about Solomon's son, Rehoboam, who was newly installed as king. One of his first decisions was to address the unrest across portions of the kingdom. He had sought guidance from his father's advisors who had experience with governing the nation. Ignoring their counsel, he went to his own advisors whom he had grown up with, likely his friends. His friends' advice was for the king to wield his power over the people and force submission. The harsh response resulted in the rebellion that split the kingdom. Advisors who have gained experience over time will likely have greater wisdom. Advisors who have less experience and possibly less wisdom may provide inadequate suggestions. Worst case scenario is if they lack the specific wisdom needed, they may tell you what you want to hear which is likely what happened with Rehoboam.

Rule 28: LOST OPPORTUNITIES

Consider the task or opportunity before you, and if you have any concerns or questions seek out the knowledge from other resources. If your research is not revealing valuable information, it may be better to engage in the task and learn as you go. Wisdom is being well-informed, but not stuck in analysis-paralysis.

Opportunities are often lost by taking too long to think about it. A wise person researches well, decides quickly, and takes action which is to manage their time well.

There will always be new situations that we have never faced before. Typically, we utilize a combination of our past experiences and knowledge and deductive reasoning to arrive at a potential solution. When we face a situation whereby we lack the knowledge or experience we can still attempt to determine a solution. When that does not work, you need to consider ways to fill in the gaps of knowledge that you are missing. Often, you can research the situation and ascertain knowledge which may lead to a solution. Attempting solutions on limited knowledge or not enough research may cost you more time than you have available and therefore miss out on an opportunity.

If you have time to make a decision, you should take the time. However, most opportunities are fleeting and as a result the timing to capture success is limited. Therefore, as the rule states: research well, decide quickly, and take action. With all the information that is at our fingertips today via the Internet on our computers and phones, it is easy to be overwhelmed with data. With all this data, "analysis paralysis" is more common than ever because our desire is to always make the perfect decision. The immense amount of data from the Internet may yield multiple potential solutions, but because of this we may still be paralyzed in our decision making. Utilize wisdom and knowledge, make the decision and move forward.

When you do not have conclusive data to make a decision, you cannot wait forever hoping for more data or you may miss the opportunity. Consider changing your approach and do not worry about hitting the bullseye on the first attempt, sometimes the approach is, "Ready ... Fire ... Aim." Sometimes you must take a shot based on the best targeting data you have at the time; make the best decision at that moment in time. Then analyze your results, adjust your plan, and take a second shot thereby learning as you go.

Many years ago, I was snowmobiling with friends in the mountains of New Mexico and we happened upon a coyote. We decided to follow the coyote but soon the coyote turned onto a new path and then another, trying to lose us. Each time the coyote turned, the first snowmobile could not react fast enough, but one of the following snowmobiles would take up the lead in the chase. After a few minutes, the coyote finally left the well-worn path and headed through the brush. We were left behind; the coyote had won. Often in life, people try solving a solution by doing what they have always done. If we repeat our same steps why should we expect a different result? The coyote finally chose a completely different direction as a solution, and sometimes we too need to take a different approach.

Like the coyote in the story, you may need to leave the well-worn path and choose a new direction. It may not be relying on yourself but reaching out for the counsel and guidance of an expert. The book of Proverbs has numerous verses telling us to seek wisdom and wise counsel.

> "Get good advice and you will succeed; don't go charging into battle without a plan." Proverbs 20:18 (GNT)

Many Churches and especially pastors have a Church board or council to guide them. Effective boards include people of various professional backgrounds and often are members of the congregation. The board can provide guidance as well as ensure that the pastor stays in touch with the congregation. Corporations have their leadership team and a board of directors to provide guidance and ensure the company and its vision are aligned. Many management books talk about professionals having their own board of directors, a team of people possessing wisdom in various areas to provide guidance in your pursuits and career. In each of these examples, leaders are receiving wisdom that will help them continue to be effective.

When you need advice and wisdom, do not hesitate too long or you may miss your window of opportunity.

Rule 33: THE VALUE OF YOUR NETWORK

Be careful who you choose as your acquaintances and friends because they will impact your reputation and success. Distance yourself from those that are uneducated, uncivilized, rude, or cruel because you may be pulled down to their level.

"Do not go where evil people go. Do not follow the example of the wicked. Don't do it! Keep away from evil! Refuse it and go on your way." Proverbs 4:14-15 (GNT)

Strive to make friends and acquaintances with people of good character and intelligence. Great friends and a strong network of acquaintances are a value to your career and your life, adding to your knowledge and reputation

CALLED TO MANAGE

An important success factor you must consider is developing an extensive and diverse network of friends, acquaintances, and professionals. We all have a network based on our current contacts, but to extend your career you should expand your network intentionally, and in the direction where you want to drive your career or in areas that you want to improve.

There are events, meetings, projects and other means to get to know people and expand your network. However, one strategic way to drive your network is to ask people to mentor you. Do not underestimate the value that ongoing and diverse mentoring can have for you. This is a way to build strong networking connections as well as learn more about other topics or careers. If you are trying to advance your knowledge in your current field, then choose a mentor from your field that you can learn and grow from. If you want to learn a new job, then choose a mentor that excels in that job area. Are there other organizations that you are interested in from a career standpoint? Then find someone to mentor you from that other organization. For example, if you wanted to consider moving into sales or marketing, then look for a mentor from one of those organizations. You may learn that those roles hold no interest for your career objectives but learning to understand how different organizations view the business can still be very valuable. Throughout all of this, you are building a network from which you can grow and leverage.

As a mentee, you need to have a short agenda or specific topic for what you want to learn from your mentor in their career or business. Be mindful that an extensive agenda may turn away potential mentors. You can always add additional topics later if the relationship is helping both parties. The agenda should keep your mentoring meetings focused and that usually results in a productive mentoring relationship. Do not be afraid to consider the unusual mentor as there may be unexpected wisdom to learn. You can benefit significantly when choosing a mentor that may be someone that you disagree with and may not even like. Unlikely mentors like these can get you out of your comfort zone and help you think outside the box. It can also be interesting and potentially a great educational experience. The relationships you build will become one of the most valuable assets you have in your life! Leverage the experience to learn and grow or leverage it to move your career in a new direction or to a new level.

As a leader, you may often find yourself mentoring others, and this too is recommended. As a mentor, it is fulfilling and rewarding to help others grow and develop in their skills and their careers. You will likely find that mentoring others helps keep the mind sharp and focused in your own professional life. You may find the mentee challenges you and you too will grow from the experience.

We have discussed mentors in our business and career but consider mentors in other aspects of your lives. In your personal life for example, you may have engaged a financial consultant which is basically a mentor. Consider how mentors can coach you with your personal growth and other mentors can help you in your spiritual life! Many Churches and organizations evangelize the need to have "small groups" whereby people become close to one another and they evolve into a personal and/or spiritual accountability group. These groups will meet on a regular basis and everyone contributes and supports one another. This includes receiving support and advice from other members. Often, these groups will have people from a variety of backgrounds with a wide range of knowledge and education. As you build deeper relationships within your group, you come to know others who have the experience and wisdom to advise you when you need help. These groups will likely have people who can help you or advise you on matters of business, personal, or spiritual issues

Rule 35: INVOLVE GOD IN YOUR DECISIONS
Include God in all your decisions at work, at home, and in the world; by being in constant prayer and studying His Word so that that Jesus Christ through the Holy Spirit will guide and direct you.

Including God in your business and in your decisions is crucial, and He is always there for you. Communicating with God comes in various forms including prayer, studying His Word, and from the support of fellow believers. Prayer is not a one-way communication avenue. Make sure to take time to listen. It may also be that we do not give God credit when it is due. Answers often pop into our minds in what seem like random chance, but why not consider how God imparts wisdom and answers to us? God may talk to you directly, send a messenger or friend, or even send a message in a dream. Do not forget, you should always consider Biblical discernment to ensure the answers align to the Word of God.

Studying the Word of God can always enlighten us to possibilities, direction, and solutions. You will find that the book of Proverbs is a book full of wisdom for your spiritual, personal, and professional life. Reading scripture may put us into the right frame of mind to hear, feel or understand God's guidance for us.

Sometimes in life we face problems or tasks that do not seem to have a solution. It brings to mind a story about dune buggy racing, one which involved a unique event that is akin to hide and seek. The event took place at night with one dune buggy hiding, and at a preset time that driver would provide a strong burst from an air horn and everyone else would start their buggies and head in the direction of the horn, trying to be the first to find the hidden buggy. After seven or eight minutes, everyone would stop and turn off their engines because every 10 minutes we would get another blast from the air horn so that we could try to zero in on the target. It was a lot of fun but driving off-road in a wooded area at night can be very challenging. You do not have a horizon or frame of reference to focus on, so it is easy to lose your sense of direction and get lost. Because of the darkness, it is easy to get so deeply stuck in the woods that you cannot seem to find a path out! Once, I was thankful when another driver came along and their headlamps combined with our own to light up the surrounding area, illuminating a path out of the woods. Or I would simply follow their lights allowing them to lead me to safety.

Communication with God whether corporately or individually will provide direction. It is a powerful tool that we too often leave out of our professional lives because we are proud and think we can solve everything ourselves. In the Bible, Job faced adversity to the point I hope no one has to face, but he remained faithful to God. In the twenty-second chapter of the book of Job, he tells us that God hears your prayers, and He will answer and shine a light onto your path. Wise counsel is like the lamp that shines on the path to give you illumination, and God's wisdom is like the dawn of day.

When you need help, you need to leverage all available resources including the wise counsel from others, and always remember God, the ultimate counselor, is always there for us!

Chapter 8:
What Is Your Plan

Do you remember when we talked about **identifying your purpose** early in the book? Well, now it is time to make that **purpose** your reality by **creating your plan**.

> *"Don't go charging into battle without a plan."* Proverbs 20:18b (GNT)

Building a plan is your next step, but this book does not provide a special planning structure for you. However, there are some basic ideas to consider when developing your plan. We will examine the eighteenth-century rules related to planning, the best practices they impart, and some shared learnings. The plan will likely need to be broken down into smaller achievable steps that align with your goal and your purpose. Plan for the entire journey and know that you may need to make adjustments in your plan along the way.

You might have a simple plan written on the back of a napkin, or you might be a project manager with a Gantt chart. Regardless, your plan should be recorded. Your plan might be written or documented digitally so that you can easily track your progress. This ensures that you are on track and allows you to develop contingency plans along the way if needed. You should also manage your stress and workload so that you do not face temptations or compromises that are not reputable.

Rule 2: PLAN
Your plan should move you towards accomplishing your purpose or goal and should be carried out in a respectable and honorable manner. Remembering that the "end" does not justify the "means."

You may have a good plan for beginning your journey, but it may be pointless if it does not fit into the larger plan to meet your purpose. Therefore, an overall and complete plan to meet your purpose should be developed.

As you develop your plan, it should obviously align with your purpose. You should also consider that each step of your plan should always move you in the direction of your purpose. Your plan is a journey in which you will reach and surpass various milestones along the way. If your plan or step is not aligned with your purpose, then you may be headed in the wrong direction and potentially moving farther away from your final goal. You must ensure that your plan does not derail your efforts within your family, personal and especially your spiritual journey. You are not successful if you simultaneously fail in the other aspects of your life.

Have you ever been part of a larger plan to meet a greater purpose than your own? The Appalachia

Service Project (asphome.org) is a wonderful organization which hosts large projects through the summer for youth and college students. They are extremely organized, planning for twelve weeks of summer projects for local homeowners in need. Projects take one week all the way up to the full twelve weeks or longer to complete. Typically, groups come and spend one week of the twelve-week summer session, and the Appalachia Service Project has a plan for each endeavor. One year, our team worked on a room addition to a small two-room house for a family of four. The previous team started the project and framed-up the room the week before. Our goal was to tie the roof structure into the existing house and complete the roofing. Our task was a single step of a large project and it was well planned, and it aligned with the overall goal. We were focused on our individual step in the larger plan.

You should plan for the entire journey, but that is not always possible in every situation. In the Appalachia Service Project story, we did not have the full plan but knew our portion or "step" of the plan was well established. We were well prepared to carry out the work and move the overall project towards the ultimate goal. When creating your plan, be thoughtful about your knowledge and ability to create an entire plan. There may be steps that cannot be fully known until some of the preceding steps are completed. You could spend more time trying to research your steps compared to actually completing them. You will likely have a basic idea for all the steps in your journey, and while it may be best to do that, the steps may not always be fully developed at the beginning. Remember that your steps should continue to move you toward your purpose.

Rule 27: CONSIDER CONSEQUENCES

Consider any consequences in all that you do in order to avoid any wrongdoing or taking on more than you can handle.

You may need to research the task because what looks easy may not be, and you can choose a better time, develop a better plan, or determine it is not worthwhile.

Taking on more than you can handle may create high stress levels and may also result in failure. It may also drive us to take shortcuts that are not honorable; the end does not justify the means. There may also be shortcuts that are worthwhile, such as consulting an expert to assist in completing the task. Why should we "reinvent the wheel" when it has already been invented and we can advance our plan through leveraging the knowledge of others? Reinventing anything that already exists is a waste of time unless you can make it better.

> "If one of you is planning to build a tower, you sit down first and figure out what it will cost, to see if you have enough money to finish the job." Luke 14:28 (GNT)

Referring to the scripture above, you need to consider the cost to complete your plan and achieve your goal. Realizing that the cost associated is also going to include the time and effort you must invest into your plan. In your planning, you need to consider how to handle situations that seem challenging or insurmountable. You may need to break this portion of the plan into smaller steps, or it may be that step where you need to engage additional resources.

We cannot anticipate everything that will happen along the way as we execute our plan. Many years back I led the preparations for a new product rollout for the company I worked for. The responsibilities included overseeing the "new product" training needs for our staff. The product rollout was scheduled for October, so we scheduled training to begin in early September. There was an internal team responsible for creating the curriculum and they utilized four project managers and eight technical writers. The team planned to finish the curriculum by the beginning of September. I disagreed with their plan and insisted that we have a "test" delivery of the training curriculum in late July, finally settling for early August. The time came for the "test" delivery of our training curriculum. It was almost a complete failure. We pulled additional staff off their current work, those who had strong writing skills, and refocused them on rewriting our curriculum. After much stress and some overtime, the new curriculum was completed prior to the rollout. Our staff worked with the project managers to create good quality curriculum in the five remaining weeks. Training classes began on time, and we were able to prepare our teams in time for the rollout. By insisting that the plan include the "test" delivery of the training curriculum, we avoided a critical situation and even failure.

You will not succeed on every step of your plan; there will be failures. It may be critical for your plan to include contingencies for failures along the way. In the launch-training story, I did not have a contingency plan, but I did include a checkpoint or evaluation along the way to ensure the plan was progressing successfully. Similarly, with the Appalachian Service Project, the Construction Coordinator had a contingency plan whereby some of our work could be rescheduled for the next work team. If we were ahead of schedule, then future steps could be pulled forward for our team. You should constantly evaluate and readjust along the way, remember the shooting analogy in the last chapter: Ready, Fire, and then Aim!

Have you created your plan that will move you towards success in your purpose? Is it aligned with your purpose? Does it sustain and support your personal, family, and spiritual efforts? Is it documented and broken down into achievable steps that can be measured based on progress and time to completion? Remember to be flexible and open to making adjustments to keep forward momentum. Do not forget to pray for and to be open to God's wisdom and guidance. Now that you have **identified your purpose** and **created your plan**, the next section is about **taking action**.

> *"Ask the Lord to bless your plans, and you will be successful in carrying them out."* Proverbs 16:3 (GNT)

PART 3: Your Action

CALLED TO MANAGE

Chapter 9: Overwhelmed

Being overwhelmed is related to how we cope with the various aspects of life and so no two people are overwhelmed by the exact same level of conditions. Have you ever noticed that when you are in a stressful situation your energy is exhausted quickly? At age sixteen, I had my first experience at off-road dune buggy racing, head-to-head with other racers. My boss was competing on a one-and-a-half-mile course and he was having a number of technical issues. Being well behind the pack, he offered me the opportunity to complete the race and gain some experience. I jumped at the chance, got my helmet, buckled-up, and off I went. After only a half lap, I noticed my arms were aching. It took me a few moments but realized that I was so tense that I was causing my own exhaustion. I shook it off and mentally told myself to relax and was able to finish the race.

Stress drains us physically and mentally at an accelerated rate. In our business world we have completely different sets of conditions and influences, but it is how we cope with these situations that determines the level of stress we feel. There will always be stress in our lives, but you must work to determine the tipping point between a reasonable level and too much stress.

Rule 17: DO NOT TAKE ON TOO MUCH
Do not attempt to take more business than you can handle. Ignoring this guideline leads a person to stress and frustration, and your problems will impact your family and friends.

Are you a person that always agrees to take on extra tasks and work? Do you dive so deeply into the business that you believe you are too essential for your job to be at risk? As discussed in chapter 2, do you seek job security to the point of being a workaholic? Does it drive you to take on too much work so that you can prove yourself in front of others? If you recognize yourself in any of these descriptions, then you might be a "people pleaser" (the person who cannot say no).

Rule #17 talks about the impact that taking on more than you can handle can have on family and friends, and it is so true. First, if we are overloaded with work we will take more time to get our job done and that time must come from somewhere else. Taking on too much work can be overwhelming and stressful but add on top of this the demands we have from the personal aspects of our lives. Increased work time will mean decreased time for God, family, and friends. Being a "people pleaser" and taking on more than you can handle can be a problem in your work life as well as your personal and spiritual lives.

CALLED TO MANAGE

When your balance is too heavy on work and the stress levels are increasing, you need a stress-relieving activity. If you have deprioritized balance within your personal life, you may not find a sufficient relief valve for your stress. Stress can continue to build and can cause physical, mental, emotional and relationship issues. These issues may add to your stress levels further and could lead to more destructive methods of coping with the stress such as alcohol, drugs, or other poor behaviors.

If we work too much, what are we sacrificing and taking time away from? Typically, it is our family that suffers most from our decisions but additionally, and maybe even worse, is that our spiritual life also suffers. Our spiritual life may become non-existent. While reduced time with family impacts your relationship with them, have you thought about the negative impact that your decreased spiritual life will have on you and your family? Also mentioned in chapter 2, my dad had a mental breakdown and went into the hospital for two years. Due to the stress of the situation, our family no longer went to Church and spirituality was placed on the backburner. The lack of spiritual guidance resulted in poor decisions for the next ten years until I began to build my relationship with God.

There is another aspect whereby many of us place undue pressure upon ourselves. Some of us tend to be perfectionists and find that we spend inordinate amounts of time on tasks that are not that important and do not really require high levels of precision. It should have been an easy task or reasonable workload, but because we spend more time than needed, we find ourselves overloaded and stressed. As a manager, we also feel responsible for everyone else's work. We spend time inspecting an employee's work, and sometimes we take over and complete it to ensure it is done right. That is more pressure that we bring upon ourselves. Perfectionism can be tied to the need for security and therefore drives us to worry about everything. A scripture passage with a simple story though difficult to follow is Matthew 6:20-34. The last verse sums it up by stating;

> *"So do not worry about tomorrow; it will have enough worries of its own."* - Matthew 6:34a (GNT).

Your work-life balance will not be the same as anyone else's, but you must find that unique individual balance from which the personal and spiritual aspects of your life can provide relief. This may include spending more time with family or with God or both. While these parts of your life will have stresses of their own, it still provides a break from the pressures of your work life. In order to keep a balance, you must learn to say "no" when appropriate so that you do not get overburdened with more work than you can reasonably handle. It can be difficult to say "no" when a co-worker or friend asks you for help, especially if you are very capable of the task. However, know that the world will not come to an end if you say "no" to someone.

Have you found that prayer can help to calm your nerves before a business engagement or negotiation? Many years ago, I was driving to a job interview for a great position and opportunity. It was pouring down rain, and I was driving on a major highway in a compact pickup truck when it started to hydroplane. I carefully counteracted the drift but could not maintain control. I spun across three lanes of the highway, twenty yards of highway shoulder and grass, and two more lanes of the access road. During the entire ordeal, I did not strike anything. The truck came to a stop facing the wrong direction with traffic coming toward me, so I quickly turned around and carefully headed on to my job interview. I am vigilant about being early, and fortunately this vigilance gave me several minutes to compose myself prior to the interview. I took a few deep breaths and I prayed! And, after praying some more, I went inside and won over the interviewers and landed the best job of my life.

Prayer is communication with God but should be much deeper. It should be a conversation with God based on a personal relationship. We always feel better when we can talk about problems with someone we trust, and with prayer we have God twenty-four-seven. You can share anything and everything with God because He understands you and your situation. He is the ultimate confidant and encourager. You can share the most difficult and painful experiences with Him, there is nothing He does not already know. He wants you to lay it all out on the table for Him, to open yourself to Him at greater levels than ever. He can help carry our burdens or even take them. We are not alone in life, whether at work or home or in the world. No matter how crazy our lives have gotten, nor how much anger we have, nor how much we have sinned, God will forgive us and always love us. Have an open conversation with God. No matter what, God loves you!

Does your team cause you stress? Sure, they do. On the flip side, do we cause our direct reports stress due to the work pressures we place on them? You are accountable for the quality of work that is produced by your team; therefore, you want to ensure that they are performing at the highest levels possible. So, are you the cause for the team to feel like they are overwhelmed? Are they trying to deal with high levels of stress the same as you? We must be cognizant of our team's physical and emotional state so that we are not the cause of their burn-out. Losing people from our teams will increase the stress on us as managers as well as that of the team members. Are you struggling with impending burn-out in your work life? Have you stopped to determine the priorities in each area of your life including your work life, your personal life, and your spiritual life?

You should know what your work priorities are, but what about the other areas of your life? Review where you make investments in your personal life. Does your investment in family make sense compared to the investment in friends or personal activities? You have the power to choose where you make the greatest investments. Are they affirming and constructive, or selfish and destructive? If you are already very stressed in your work life and possibly on the verge of burn-out, then personal activities that are destructive will only add to your overall level of stress and burn-out.

Where are you in your spiritual life? Are you spending time focusing on God, or are you living a self-centered existence? If you live a self-centered existence and you are stressed to the point of burn-out, then you have nothing else to leverage to help you in your situation. If you are invested in your spiritual life, then you have the God of the universe to call on for help. He gives love, provides wisdom, and can bring you peace as no one else can. You can call on God to help you in every aspect of your life – your spiritual life, your personal life, and even in your work life. Do not forget about this infinite resource available to you when you are stressed with work!

Rule 25: MANAGING OVERWHELMING WORK
If you receive more business than you can handle, do not panic, but prioritize your work and complete each task step by step.

If you are busy and someone brings you additional work, do you start to panic and become anxious? When you experience this situation, does it take you a long time to calm down and approach the problem logically? For some of us, when we are in a situation such as this our panic and anxiety may manifest itself emotionally. The emotions alone can be a challenge to control, and even more so as managers who are looked upon by directs for leadership. We cannot allow our emotions to become uncontrolled. We must calm ourselves down and face the problem.

Again, prioritization is important as we dissect the work into smaller actions or tasks and then simply arrange them in the order of their priority. The only exception is if some tasks have a dependency on another to be complete. There are numerous ways to prioritize. For example, we could approach our tasks based on a descending order of categories: <u>Important & Urgent</u>, <u>Important & Not Urgent</u>, <u>Not Important & Urgent</u>, and <u>Not Important & Not Urgent</u> (These are based on the Eisenhower principle for decision making).

The idea is to develop a step-by-step plan to tackle the workload. The first step of your journey through this project is to focus on the first item or step. Like a marathon or an expedition, you start with the first step followed by the second, and so on. Take one step or one item at a time. This is not earth-shattering news to anyone. We just need to develop our plan and then execute it.

Studies have revealed that multitasking is not efficient, except maybe when one of your tasks is something rote or practically done via muscle memory. An example would be driving a car while talking on the phone. If you suddenly face an unusual driving situation, you will have to shift your attention to the road and miss parts of your conversation. Focus on one item or one step at a time because switching between tasks takes time in itself. Turn off or eliminate any distractions that interfere with you completing your work.

Rule 31: KEEP EMOTIONS UNDER CONTROL

Keep your emotions under control and do not let excessive emotion control you. Decisions should be made with a balance of emotion, thought and reason. Emotions are a wonderful gift to us from God. However, excessive emotions or emotional outbursts may lead to hurting yourself, hurting friends, angering others, creating enemies, or cause you to lose the of respect of others.

Emotions are a gift from God that can make our world and our lives beautiful. Emotions manifest in a behavior which will vary from person to person. For example, happiness may cause them to laugh out loud. However excessive and/or uncontrolled emotions can have a very different effect, potentially causing a negative behavior.

We have all heard stories of leaders that erupt at bad news or a bad situation and as a result those who work for them live in fear. The fear is because they do not want to be the cause of the leader's next outburst. This causes reduced communication and a reduction in ideas and strategy. It may also hide bad situations until they turn into a crisis, perhaps one that cannot be resolved.

Does your anger expose itself in outbursts of temper, or do you swallow it and let it eat away at you on the inside? Both have adverse effects on us. Unfortunately, I inherited my father's temper but have learned to control it most of the time. When I do lose my temper, I am stricken with embarrassment and shame. Those who witness outbursts of anger are put off by it, especially anyone who was the target of the anger.

When this happens, the reputation that we have managed to build with our directs and coworkers is going take a hit. Some damage to our reputation may never be restored, and therefore others may forever view us with diminished respect.

A lot of parents raise their children to be strong and independent. In the context of business, it is often a dog-eat-dog world and again we are driven to succeed independently. If we have success, we are tempted to become full of selfish pride and possibly arrogance. However, life has a way of throwing curve balls at us and bringing us down a notch. Is your character strong enough to handle all that life throws at you? I believe that no one can handle everything life throws at them with perfect emotional poise and control.

Anger and pride together can be especially destructive because we may not allow ourselves to seek forgiveness and restoration in our relationship with those whom we have hurt. Anger and pride are probably strong traits for a dictator, which should make us stop and consider our actions more closely. As leaders, we should seek to be a servant for others and seek humility so that our relationships are strengthened. If you lose your temper, do you go back and apologize for your actions?

When you are overwhelmed with stress does it affect your personality and emotional state? Does the stress result in anger, depression, or emotionally falling apart? You can also make the choice to act and tackle your problems but undertaking that alone can bring added stress. Seek to reduce the stress you are experiencing by removing factors or by adding resources. Consider seeking the support of others, and you should always seek the support of God through a personal relationship. We are loved by God and we are not alone!

CALLED TO MANAGE

Chapter 10:
Get Help and Manage

In the last chapter we discussed how at times we become overwhelmed, and often that may come from having more work than we can handle. The excess work may be a result of increased business or opportunities, or it may be related to correcting business issues. Regardless of the reason, it must be addressed so that we continue to move forward in business. When you feel overloaded, you need to ask for help. There is a great example of Moses asking God for help in managing the millions of Hebrews in their exodus from Egypt:

> *So he asked, "LORD, why have you brought me this trouble? How have I displeased you that you put the burden of all these people on me? ... I can't take care of all these people by myself. This is too much work for me!" The LORD answered Moses, "Bring me 70 Israelite men who you know are leaders and officers of the people. Take them to the tent of meeting, and have them stand with you. I'll come down and speak with you there. I'll take some of the Spirit that is on you and put it on them. They will help you take care of the people. You won't have to take care of the people alone."* Numbers 11:11,14,16-17 (GW)

We may not have the same responsibility as Moses but there comes a time when we must ask for help. While it may be easy for us to help others, most of us will let our stubborn independence and pride get in the way of asking for help to complete our own work and projects.

Rule 29: GET HELP WHEN NEEDED
Do not miss a time-base opportunity or a deadline when you need help, do not delay in calling upon trusted and capable people to accomplish the needed tasks.

When asking for help, you will need to manage their work well so that they are efficient and accomplish their work effectively.

Also, in the last chapter we talked about being inundated with more work than you can initially handle. We talked about calming down and prioritizing that work, but what do you do when there is still more work than you can handle? We cannot "freeze-up" and do nothing, and we cannot allow procrastination to set in. We must take action. Prioritizing is still an important step, but decisions must be made, and they may include bringing in more resources to help you with that work whether temporary or long-term. In the United States, we have held up individual "independence" as an important part of our freedom, but sometimes it can get in our way. We let our stubborn independence and pride get in the way and we feel weak if we must ask someone else for help. We cannot let pride keep us from making prudent decisions that could ultimately grow our business. We must be willing to ask for help when we need it.

If the overflow of work is temporary, then you may only want to bring in people temporarily as a short-term solution. Can you borrow resources or get someone to pitch in for short-term projects? Otherwise you may need to contract for temporary workers. Realize that for this type of help they will need more guidance from you to understand the tasks that you need them to complete. You may be able to delegate all the easier aspects of the work to the temp staff thereby reducing the amount of management needed from you. Depending on the complexity of work, the staff you contract with will likely need to be commensurate with the work to be done. Cutting corners or saving costs on temp staffing may cost you much more in the longer term because it will require more supervision from you. However, temporary staffing helps to optimize your budget and allows you to complete your work without a long-term investment in fulltime employees.

Another short-term solution is to consider sub-contracting a piece of the work needing to be done. This will likely be a more expensive means to get the work done, however if it is for the mid-term or long-term, then it could be a very viable alternative. Another possibility is if a piece of work you need done requires specialized skills or equipment, then it may be less expensive to contract with another business to complete this portion of the work.

If the work is long-term or permanent, then you might consider hiring a fulltime employee as your solution. In this situation you can train them to help with the current tasks, but as they learn and grow it will take less supervision from you. There will always be some level of supervision and training so that they can perform new tasks and provide additional support for the work you do as your business evolves and changes. Direct reports that are fulltime employees are a long-term investment and they can help you and your team be more productive and more successful.

Another solution which can be very helpful is using a mixture of short-term and long-term tactics, especially if you have uncertain or seasonal demands in your business. Your fulltime direct reports will be there all year, but the temp staff are available to help you meet those unexpected demands or the seasonal staffing needs of your business. To relieve pressure from you and potentially provide learning opportunities to your fulltime direct reports, you can have them supervise the work of the temporary staff.

If you have a time-based business opportunity, analyze the needs, make the decision, and get started so that you can capitalize on the opportunity.

Rule 23: DO YOUR OWN WORK, GET HELP IF NEEDED

If God has equipped you to easily complete your tasks, then do so. Do not risk the quality or timely completion by giving the task to someone who has not already earned your trust.

However, you may want to provide a work opportunity for another person and the goodwill you provide may be more important than your own pride.

If you can easily perform the work needed, then do so. However, if you need help, make the decision and move forward so that you can take advantage of business that may not come around again. No one knows your individual business like yourself, so when you have analyzed the need, do not fear making the decision.

New or complex opportunities may be perfect to delegate to a direct report because it will give them an opportunity to grow and develop their own capabilities. In this situation the goodwill garnered will be the respect and loyalty to you from your direct report. Most people want to advance their careers and gain additional wisdom from the experiences you can provide for them that will help them on their journey. Their wisdom grows from expanding their knowledge, and they will also learn from their failures if you take the time to lead them through the failure to eventual success. In addition to serving as a learning experience for your direct report, it could also be a step towards succession planning so that you can turn more and more of the business over to your fulltime direct report and free yourself up to pursue other opportunities.

The goodwill provided for temporary staffing will likely be the opportunity for them to simply earn some money. They will likely already have the basic skills necessary to perform the work, so growing their skills may not earn any goodwill. However, if the temporary staff is in an internship program for which they are trying to learn the business, the goodwill will come from giving them the opportunity to learn the business, grow their skills, and still earn a little money.

CALLED TO MANAGE

Rule 18: DO NOT MEDDLE

Do not interfere with another person's issues except to lend your support to sincerely help that person. Sticking your nose in another's business is considered unacceptable.

> *"Also, make it your goal to live quietly, do your work, and earn your own living."* 1 Thessalonians 4:11 (GW)

Sometimes it is easier for us to help others than to allow someone to help us. When it comes to our business, we can be protective and even defensive of our domain. Sometimes we do not allow people to help us because we may not want them to get into our business and potentially tell us what to do.

If someone has asked you for help, then you should focus on providing them the help they need for that moment in time. Telling them how they could have done it better, or improvements they could have made, or what mistakes they previously made that caused them to be behind in their business is NOT helping them. I am not saying that providing advice is bad, but there is a time and place for it as well as a method. What does this person need now? Their business or situation is overwhelming them, and they first need to get the pressure off. We should diligently and sincerely help them to correct their problem so that they can find relief.

> *"Whenever you possibly can, do good to those who need it. Never tell your neighbors to wait until tomorrow if you can help them now."* Proverbs 3:27-28 (GNT)

CALLED TO MANAGE

No one listens well when overwhelmed, but once they have found relief, they will be more receptive to your wisdom and counsel. Even if they still may not be receptive, you earned some respect and freedom by helping them through their dilemma. Remember, they may still feel battered and injured from the experience and will likely be sensitive to it. If you respect and love your neighbor who was struggling, you will need to be very careful in giving your advice. Provide appropriate and thoughtful guidance, delivering it in a gentle and supportive manner. Keep in mind what you would be open to hearing if you were in their situation.

Similarly, we should be mindful of others meddling in our business whether externally or internally. We can typically control influence that is coming from outside our business because we can cut off that communication. However, the meddling could be coming from your direct reports, partners or peers in the business and that is much more challenging to manage.

Let us pause for a moment and talk about the difference between meddling and valuable advice. When we receive uninvited suggestions or directives, we will likely want to put up our defenses and repel the intrusion into our business. However, we must take a moment to discern whether they are unmerited and erroneous suggestions, intentional and damaging assertions, or potentially valuable counsel. Throughout the book of Proverbs, we are instructed to listen and to understand the wisdom and counsel given us. However, there is an appropriate time and place to provide advice and you may need to respond to the person with a suggested time to meet and discuss.

If the meddling is coming from an internal source, you should confront the person or persons directly and quickly. I believe you should first determine the motivation behind their meddling so that you can ascertain if it was intended to be helpful or hurtful to the business. If it was to intentionally hurt the business, then the problem needs to be corrected immediately and could include severing the relationship with that person. It does not matter if you are currently in a season of calm or chaos, if they are left within the business, they can be a poison that spreads across the entire team and further diminishes overall productivity. If this person had good intentions but was wrong, it will be valuable to spend a little time with that person. The learning opportunity for them will build loyalty and respect for your leadership, and they will be more knowledgeable and therefore focus on the right goals. It may also be a learning opportunity for you, because while the person may not be correct, they may provide valuable insight to you about a piece of the business where they live every day. If their meddling turns out to be good advice, you will learn and grow from it.

We control who and where our help comes from and we should always be open and mindful of Biblical guidance.

Chapter 11:
Managing Up vs. Politics

"Managing up" and "politics" in the workplace are similar activities but with completely different approaches and intentions. Everyone needs a good connection with their superiors, and "managing up" is an approach implemented with integrity. In comparison, the "politics" approach is often accomplished without integrity, however there are important aspects as well.

You need to build a strong relationship with your superiors, so that your work is always aligned to the business strategy. The strong relationship is also needed so that you can provide your management with information about your work, especially regarding aspects that directly impact them or their strategies. You must own the relationship to ensure your best interests are served and communicated because your manager may or may not take any initiative to help you with your work or career. You must understand how to communicate with your manager. How do they want to receive information or messages? There are numerous training classes and strategies on how best to communicate with others that you might consider, but these will not be covered in this book. But do know that open communication is necessary and allows for feedback from your manager that may provide you with guidance and even course correction before you go too far off track.

Every manager you have will be different and you must determine how to make it work. You are like a project manager keeping your stakeholders informed, meeting their expectations, while you move the project forward. Everyone considers the "WIIFM" (What's In It For Me?), and your managers and stakeholders are no different. How can you best help your manager be successful? This will likely include success for you and your team as well. Have you talked with your manager about how you might help them meet their goals and land their projects? You may also be in a situation where you are working more autonomously, and your boss may not have as much time for you. Sometimes in those situations you might take the approach to "be brief, be bright, be gone." You will obviously need to be prepared so that you can be brief and bright. You need to make sure you include the "ask" so that your boss can make the decision and you can exit quickly and let them get on with their business.

Managing up and building a relationship with your management will be beneficial and might help you avoid pitfalls. However, you may also find yourself managing up into political situations, or you find that others are driving their political agenda with your manager. As a manager, your employees may promote their own political agendas to you. Be very mindful about the information coming to you from your direct reports.

Use discernment to determine the validity of the data as well as the motivation behind it, if any. Do not be blinded by someone who is telling you what you want to hear and are praising you in order to apply undue influence.

You might recall that I managed an automobile service department, which also happened to be a privately-owned dealership. At one point I had hired a new service advisor, then a couple of days later the owner's son told me that I needed to hire a family friend. I stated that I had already chosen the best candidate and that person had already given notice to their current employer. I did not budge on my decision. A few months later, the owner had to sell off one of his dealerships that his son was managing. The owner's son brought in the service manager from that other dealership and replaced me.

Politics in the workplace can be helpful or hurtful depending on where the "party" lines are drawn. Because we can never know when a shift in power can happen, it may be best to stay out of any destructive politics as much as possible. Selfish ambition drives people to get ahead regardless of the cost for them and for others. Some definitions of politics use the word devious, and you may or may not have experienced that. You will find that those who practice selfish politics are extremely good at selling themselves to their managers and to higher levels of management, regardless of the truth. One way they do this is by stepping on the accomplishments of others and claiming them as their victories. The managers above typically do not engage down to the lower levels, so they are blind to the truth. They believe what they are being told by those managers that strive and survive by their political ambition, and these managers appear to be strong people managers when they are not. Sometimes the frontline workers, or those workers at the lower level live in fear from that manager and will not speak out about the truth. When politics is influenced by selfish ambition, it becomes a malicious practice that is an unfortunate part of the world, but we are not part of that world as we are people of God.

No one can escape politics in the business world and whether you participate in the politics or not, you will feel an impact from it at some point. How do you handle the negative conflict from someone else's political agenda? You might become angry with the perpetrator or others involved, which may not help the situation. Some people will fall into the trap of the "victim mentality." As the victim, you allow and even accept the troubles that happen to you, and you will likely fall into self-pity. You have blindly accepted that someone else will rule over your life influencing your reactions, thoughts, and outlook.

Political agendas may impact and shape decisions and processes in our workplace, but they do NOT rule over us! You can control how you react and how you manage through the situation, and as a result this will influence your attitude. Responding in self-pity or anger may take the negative situation and make it worse. As leaders, your reactions and outward feelings will further influence all your direct reports and how they too react to the situation. Political circumstances can be highly volatile and could result in you or your direct reports losing their jobs.

If the political situation originates from high above, then you may have little influence to change the situation itself, but again you can control how you and your team move forward. If the situation or decision comes from your direct manager and depending on your relationship with them, you can engage them in discussion about it. If your peers feel similarly, then maybe as a group you discuss the situation with your manager. Prayerfully consider your course of action as the situation could be a volatile subject to discuss.

If you have a peer that is putting forward a political agenda, then you may need to make sure that your opinions and thoughts as well as those of your peers are also heard. You and your peers can specifically join forces because the opinion of an alliance may be more powerful than that of an individual. Remember however, that you may now be playing on their level in the political arena.

While most of the time when we hear of politics it has a negative connotation to it, but we also need to understand that politics can be a positive term as well. An old joke states that you can understand the word politics by breaking it down to the two parts of the word: poly meaning many, and ticks meaning blood sucking organisms. But in its most literal sense, Webster's defines politics as the debate and competition among groups or individuals for the purpose of power through leadership and control, especially in governments. It is also defined as the efforts that continue further influencing, winning over or maintaining control of power. The key concepts when relating to office politics are the debate and power aspects. When a decision needs to be made, it is usually made by reaching adequate consensus to sway the balance of power to one side or the other. Great accomplishments can be made if you can learn how to align the key power brokers behind your ideas and work with each of the factions to make sure they get something they wanted. This is how democracy worked for the founding fathers.

Are you caught up in destructive politics or productive politics? As people leaders, we should manage Biblically and must not lead anyone astray.

Rule 19: DO NOT ENGAGE IN CONTROVERSY
Do not get involved in public or private organizational disagreements further than you are spiritually or legally required so that you are not caught in the middle and lose.

"This is why I always try to do what I believe is right before God and before everyone." Acts 24:16 (ERV)

Your mind will be at ease because you are not at fault for the resulting dissention, which will bring you peace.

Politics often include controversy, and how you manage and deal with controversy will be seen by others. Their observations will be another piece of data in how people view you and your character as a leader. There will be times that you must fight the good fight and to do what is right based on your beliefs.

However, fighting for a decision that you cannot win may cause sympathy and support to shift towards the decision proposed by another group. The other group's goals may not align with your goals. In debating your point of view, you have essentially laid all your cards out on the table and you may be at a disadvantage. This other group will have learned from the points you presented and can better prepare their position and defend their case going forward. If you are not properly equipped to take on the fight, then you should find a way to equip yourself with appropriate resources for the situation. For example, if the fight was to be waged in a courtroom and you are not a lawyer, then you will likely need the legal wisdom of a lawyer.

We must live in the worldly environment that surrounds us, but as Christians we are not to conform to it. In some circumstances, we can change our environment by changing jobs, companies, or moving to live under a different government. The Bible tells us to submit to rulers and authorities, obeying them if it does not contradict the Bible. Rulers and authorities include governments, world leaders, as well as management and supervisors. In the face of adversity, we are to show kindness and love which will have its own influence over those who are against us.

"If your enemies are hungry, feed them; if they are thirsty, give them a drink. You will make them burn with shame, and the Lord will reward you." Proverbs 25:21-22 (GNT)

Sometimes those with political ambition will win the battle, and they leave casualties in their wake. Casualties may be minor, or they may be major such as people losing their job. Whatever the situation, look to God to give you strength to face your adversities. Lean on Him to stand strong, staying above the muck and mire so that you maintain your faith, character and integrity.

Rule 12: LIFE OF INTEGRITY
Be that man of high integrity so that others may see and respect you for these traits and your "word" will carry influence. If you talk about integrity but do not live it, then others will find out and you will be considered unreliable.

"If you make a promise to God, keep your promise. Don't be slow to do what you promised. God is not happy with fools. Give God what you promised to give him." Ecclesiastes 5:4 (ERV)

Throughout this book, we have been talking about what makes you who you are. Do not let politics and adversity make you into something you are not! Have you ever lost or been defeated, but something good came out of it? In the beginning of this chapter, I told my story of having been pushed out of my role as service department manager for a new car dealership. I had led the dealership from less-than-average quality rating to being number one in our sales region. I had earned the respect of the manufacturer's representative, and it was this representative that directed me to another opportunity as a service department manager. Had I not maintained my character and integrity throughout the entire ordeal of being replaced, it is likely that the new opportunity would not have come.

You may lose political battles but know that God will win in the end.

CALLED TO MANAGE

Chapter 12:
Take Action

A common quote used for centuries states, "A journey of a thousand miles begins with a single step," (Confucius). Beginning a journey with your first step is the same with executing on your plan. The key is ... you must take that first step!

> **Rule 3: ACTION**
> When you have an honorable purpose and a worthy plan, there comes a time to stop planning and take action. Be decisive and persistent in carrying out your "Action Plan."
>
> There is no admiration for someone who devised a great plan but never acted on it.
>
> *"If we do not do the good we know we should do, we are guilty of sin."* James 4:17 (GNT)

Stop mulling over your plan and take the first step into action. One of the challenges that manufacturing companies face are customers who believe that the product should be perfect and free of defects. The problem with this is that companies would never rollout complex new products because it will never be defect free. As we discussed in chapter 8, you may not ever finalize your plan end-to-end, but you need to launch into action taking that first step!

Rule 24 Part 1: PROCRASTINATION
Do not put off until tomorrow the work you can complete today, else the value of that work may diminish by an unnecessary delay.

"Work hard at whatever you do." Ecclesiastes 9:10a (GNT)

Have you ever been in a meeting in which discussion has dragged on, and then the issue is tabled to a later date? We often walk away from these meetings feeling like people were afraid to make a decision. To move forward you may have to push people to make decisions in order to move forward, but this is not the norm that we are used to. Many people avoid making decisions for various reasons and sometimes it may be warranted, but sometimes it may be due to procrastination or fear. Procrastination can be used as a rationale for not taking action or not moving forward toward your goals. Many people struggle with procrastination to a point it becomes a habit, but you should seek to understand why it prevents you from starting on your endeavors.

Do you delay decisions using various rationales, for example you believe you do not have time? This is a very common reason for procrastinating, and a rationalization that I myself am guilty of using when writing this very book. I have put this book off for years until it finally felt like God's calling was urgent. I still went through cycles of procrastination and stopped writing for a few weeks until feeling the urgency again. Then I prioritized time to spend on writing another chapter or portion of a chapter. What are you prioritizing above moving forward to accomplish your goals and dreams? Could you reduce the time you spend watching television or other activity? Do not eliminate these altogether because there will be days when you are stressed or exhausted and need time to simply relax. You must still overcome your procrastination and take a step forward toward your goal.

Fear is another common obstacle that people wrestle with, and more specifically a fear of failure. It is easy to say that we should learn from our failure, but we still fear failure. And if we do fail, we should absolutely learn from every mistake and miscalculation. Then we become better educated to face similar issues going forward in our plan and throughout our lives. Fear may be related to the task itself or even of being successful. Regardless, we should not allow fear to dictate our lives or our next step toward our goal.

Life also provides numerous distractions from our daily work and personal lives. We find that some part of our life is too overwhelming or consuming for us to focus on our plan. If your goal is to better yourself in your work life or personal life, then you need to find the time to execute your plan. You might need to carve out enough time to enable you to complete a single step so that you can still make progress toward your goal. Concentrate on taking that first step in your plan, or the next step if you have already started your journey.

It is easy to talk yourself out of accomplishing your goals by diminishing the goal's value compared to your current situation or even dismissing it completely. You might encounter others who will dismiss your plan or goals as not attainable or just a pure dream. There could also be internal and external forces that will work against you or your journey to reach your goal. Review your plan and look at the steps you have identified and determine if your next step or even your next few steps are attainable. If these steps move you toward your goal or purpose, then do not let the negativity hold you back. Take that next step.

In whatever situation, you cannot allow procrastination to stop you. It is easy to rationalize anything as unattainable, but typically rationalization is making the illogical sound plausible. If you are stuck in your plan, or maybe have not even started your first step, then consider making some changes. Consider breaking your next step into smaller activities that are easier, or possibly find some actions that could be considered "low hanging fruit" whereby accomplishing these might give you a quick win. Set yourself a specific timeline or deadline for completing you next step. Use a combination of options, but you must make sure to move forward taking that next step.

If you are struggling to move forward, refer back to chapter 4 and the content about being accountable to yourself. What is preventing you from taking that next step? Are there distractions or obligations in your life that need to be addressed? Similarly, in chapter 6 the focus was about being accountable to those you manage. The team is connected to your goals, so moving forward or not moving forward will impact them. You have a responsibility to lead your team in a way that will provide success, but more importantly to provide them with safety and security. A successful and productive business is more likely to provide job security for your direct reports. You must consider the priorities in your life and in your team's lives and include these in your decision making. With the tremendous responsibility placed upon you as a people leader, pray to God for wisdom, guidance, and encouragement.

Rule 26: TIME MANAGEMENT
Manage your time well so that you are prepared to take advantage of each opportunity that comes along because you may never get another chance at it.

If you are managing your time well and are prepared, you will be ready to tackle new opportunities. This is especially true if you start early and manage your time well.

Many goals are related to time-sensitive situations or possibly opportunities which are short-lived. Because of this, it is critical to act on your plan and constantly move toward your goals. Time is a valuable commodity which cannot be recovered once spent. This is why time-management is so important and why there are tens of thousands of books and courses on the subject. If you struggle with Time Management then you may want to consider books, courses or other resources that can help. At this point you should have a plan in place which is broken down into steps. Manage your time by applying timelines or deadlines for completing each of your steps. Prioritize the activities in your life to find more available time to commit to your plan. Share your plan with someone else, someone you see as a trusted advisor regarding your plan and goal. This will help create an additional accountability on staying focused on the completion of that next step.

Rule 22: WORK HARD
"Work hard and do not be lazy." Romans 12:11a (GNT)

Laziness leads to more of the same. When you know how to be productive in work and business, focus on it to completion. Not all effort will prove successful, but if you believe it to be achievable you should engage fully.

Laziness can become habitual to the point you are not motivated to better yourself or your situation. The Bible frequently speaks against laziness and goes on to state that a good person is one who is industrious. If you have a purpose or goal and you have created your plan, then you have two of the three aspects that are likely to produce success. Do not think of the daunting journey ahead of you in order to reach your goal but focus on completing the next step.

Rule 24 Part 2: HONEST WORK

You should seek an honest profit in the business you engage in so that you can support your family and provide goodwill to others. Dishonest profits or unreasonable gains may lead to business failures for a variety of reasons.

"But people who want to get rich keep falling into temptation. They are trapped by many stupid and harmful desires which drown them in destruction and ruin. Certainly, the love of money is the root of all kinds of evil." 1 Timothy 6:9-10a (GW)

A respectable and honest businessperson should be:

"Good, honest people who refuse to hurt others for money will live through that fire. They refuse to take bribes or listen to plans to murder other people. They refuse to look at plans for doing bad things." Isaiah 33:15 (ERV)

Your business profits should be honest and reasonable but resist the temptation to boost profits in a way that could lead to corruption.

As believers in God, we should never take advantage of or cheat another person. How often is the amount of gain so insignificant in the grand scheme of life? If a person must cheat others to make a profit, then their entire business model is based on deception and sin. They will likely have to continue their practice of deceit to keep the business profitable because they have not found the honest means of turning a profit.

CALLED TO MANAGE

Do you have God first in your life, and similarly have you put God first in your business or professional life? God blesses those that put Him first in their lives and in their business, but the blessings you receive may not be in monetary prosperity. God never said He would make your life easy. God is willing to walk with you throughout your life, through your mountain top experiences and your darkest valleys. He will be with you on every step of your journey to accomplish your goals and reaching for your purpose.

What step can you accomplish today? Go and take that next step!

Summary and Conclusion

CALLED TO MANAGE

Chapter 13:
Summary and Conclusion

Are you living your best life? What purpose does God have for you and your life? Consider your purpose or your current goal in the larger context of your professional life and where it intersects with your spiritual life. Your passion in life will likely align in some manner with your purpose.

As a manager, we need to have a passion for people and for helping others to be successful at reaching their potential. Typically, this is what draws people into leading and managing people. You should feel excited and blessed to see others excel in their endeavors and reach their dreams. Your professional life and spiritual life can coexist and be in alignment. In these situations, you should feel that you are fulfilling God's calling for your life. Do you feel that you are in the exact place that God wants you to be, as a child of God living in the world, and in this case the business world? If you are not able to align your professional and spiritual purpose, then you may be missing the deeper significance you can have in this world.

Do you have a plan with regard to accomplishing your purpose? Have you prayed about your plan, that it may align with God's will for you? Did you seek advice to help in formulating your plan? For most new activities you pursue you will need to have some type of plan. Your plan may be to "wing it" when figuring out the next steps needed to get you there. You may have high-level or extensively structured plans to meet your goals. Did you know that God has a plan for you, one which aligns with His calling on your life, a plan that will bring you closer to Him and that will bless your life? In the book of Jeremiah, God declares, *"I know the plans that I have for you, ... plans to give you a future filled with hope,"* Jeremiah 29:11 (GW). When you develop your plan to reach your goals or purpose, God should be an integral part in the development of your plan.

You have discovered your purpose or goal, and you developed your plan. The next phase in pursuing your purpose is taking action. We cannot procrastinate or let fears and distractions dissuade us from moving forward. Whatever obstacles you encounter, leverage all the resources available to you to overcome the challenge. The first resource is prayer. Pray for God's hand to guide you through the confrontation so that you continue toward your purpose. Are you passionate and excited in carrying out your action plan in pursuit of your goals and purpose? Typically, people who have a passion and desire for a project or their purpose are more likely to succeed. If your passion and desire is not in the tasks, is it in the goal or purpose? You may be required to complete tasks that you are not excited about, but which may be required to move you forward toward your goal which you are passionate about. If the task is not moving you toward your goal, it might be time to reflect on your plan to ensure you are moving in the right direction. There might need to be some adjustments to the plan, or you may find that you are being called to take a new direction.

God calls each of us to a specific purpose that is uniquely tailored for each person. As there were many leaders called by God in the Bible, there is a need for Godly leaders and managers in business today. However, being a Godly manager does not make us superior to anyone else. In fact, it is just the opposite. We should be a servant to others, our direct reports and our peers, including managers and individual contributors. Being a Christian manager does not mean criticizing or condemning non-Christian managers. We are called to support and love one another.

SUMMARY OF RULES 1-3
These three rules provide guidance for a successful journey towards accomplishing your purpose. Start on your "Action Plan" with energy and enthusiasm and be determined in your effort.

These guidelines will help you achieve great and highly respected accomplishments, an honorable legacy left behind and a life of great service for our God and Savior.

We may not completely accomplish our purpose or all our goals, but we must remember that our will may not align with God's will for us. In all things, God will use each of us for His good purposes.

"We know that in all things God works for good with those who love him, those whom he has called according to his purpose." Romans 8:28 (GNT)

CALLED TO MANAGE

If you think back to the three sections of this book: **Your Purpose**, **Your Plan**, and **Your Action**, you might think I departed from being a book about people leadership and management. But everything you and your team accomplishes is related to achieving your goals. As a people leader, you need to take these concepts to the next level. It is time to teach these basic principles (purpose, plan, and action) to your direct reports, helping them to identify their purpose, develop their plan, and coach them to take action.

There may be concerns about training direct reports to be so successful that their success might surpass our own. As a result, you may feel fear that you are no longer necessary to the business. All of us have likely had moments when thoughts like these cross our minds. If your manager or your company believes that you are not needed because your team is effectively handling the business, then they are indeed very short-sighted. The gift of guiding and growing direct reports to reach their maximum potential and achieving their goals is not an easy skill to develop. Your value for leading people to be better is an uncommon skill and is very valuable.

As a Godly manager, you will find it tremendously rewarding to see new direct reports develop, grow and thrive in their careers. One of my favorite stories exemplifying this was a sub-contracting project I managed which included more than four hundred people. Most of our contractors were recent college graduates pursuing their dreams and career aspirations. We had the opportunity to provide these young men and women guidance, knowledge and encouragement to succeed and reach for their goals. Almost every person had a drive and a desire to improve their own lives and situations, and it was wonderful to see success on a large scale such as this. Many landed great opportunities, radically advancing their careers. The excitement and passion in these young men and women was contagious and I found this experience to be one of the most rewarding times of my career.

The workplace needs more strong and caring people-leaders so that we keep our businesses strong and competitive in the world marketplace. Companies will promote people into a manager role or hire managers externally, and thereby the company has given that person the authority over their team of people. Authority may make you a manager, it is how you engage with your team that makes you a leader of people.

Leaders have a purpose and a vision which they share with their team, so that they too are motivated and driving towards the same goals. Because your team members are in the same organization as you their purpose and goals will typically be similarly aligned. Therefore, you and your team should be driving toward the same goals and overall success for the organization and company.

You will be blessed when you help others to be successful, helping them reach their potential or their dreams. Everyone wants to have a life of value, and as leaders our value is measured in the lives we have impacted as a Godly Manager.

CALLED TO MANAGE

I have enjoyed sharing my experiences and stories with you through this book. I hope in some way you have gained something from the time you invested in reading. I must give credit where credit is due, and that is to God for His blessings on my life, and the calling I have felt in leading people and now in sharing my experience with you. Know that God has a purpose specifically for you!

I will end with a story from Matt. 14:22-33. Jesus had already called the disciples to be in ministry with Him, and ultimately to help Him fulfill God's purpose. For the disciples, every experience with Jesus was another step in God's plan. One night the disciples were in the boat ahead of Jesus when a storm arose upon the Sea of Galilee. The disciples had fought it most of the night. Then they saw Jesus walking on the water approaching the boat. Peter saw Jesus and said if it is You, call me to come to You on the water. Jesus called Peter to come, and Peter got out of the boat and began to walk toward Jesus. Then fear of the storm distracted Peter and his faith fell short. Peter began to sink, and Jesus had to save him. While Peter had doubts, he was the only person to take that initial step out of the boat. The other disciples were fearful and afraid to take any action. Peter's faith may have fallen a little short, but he did step out of the boat. The questions for you: Are YOU ready to get out of the boat?

Are YOU ready to take **ACTION?**

Afterward:
Life Beyond Managing

Chapter 4 included the story of seeing an ambulance in front of my parents' house and the passing of my dad. The additional message from that story was that my dad passed away at age fifty-seven, very likely brought on by the stress of his current situation at the time.

> **Rule 32: MAINTAIN YOUR HEALTH**
> Keep healthy for the sake of your family, your business associates, and especially for yourself. Be thoughtful of reasonable eating and drinking, as eating or drinking to excess can lead to other problems including physical and mental issues. Living a healthier lifestyle will improve your future wellbeing.

The story of my dad's passing is important here as it supports a couple of important and relevant points. The first point is about handling stressful events in your life. The body of believers are to love and support one another, especially in tragic situations like this. My Church family responded with an outpouring of God's love for me and my family. I was blown away by the support and love I felt throughout this tragic experience. Yes, I have a wonderful and loving family, but they too were grieving for the loss of their spouse, father or grandfather. Having a Church family to support you can be a huge factor in sustaining a reasonable level of spiritual and emotional health. In life, we will face tough situations including grief, anger, depression, self-pity and other destructive forces. Everyone can benefit from a support group which likely includes your immediate family and Church family to help you maintain spiritual and emotional health.

"Peace of mind makes the body healthy." Proverbs 14:30a (GNT)

The second point relates to taking care of yourself. My dad almost never went to the doctor for check-ups or any form of health screening. Had he done so, there likely would have been treatments to keep him healthier. So, the second objective is to work on and maintain your physical health. There are many aspects of our lives that will impact our physical and mental health, and each of us should consider how to improve our situation. There are doctors and counselors who specialize in treating our mental and emotional health. God has provided doctors with the knowledge to improve our total health, including physically, mentally, and emotionally. Do you have a plan for your physical health, and are you taking action on that plan?

Rule 30: REST, RELAX AND REJUVENATE

Take you mind off work in order to rest your body and mind so that you can come back to it ready to engage well. Dwelling only on work will continually erode your strength and mental capabilities.

During times of relaxation divert your thoughts with pleasant and fulfilling forms of entertainment. Be cautious of entertainment and materials that are not healthy or uplifting because these can be damaging to your wellbeing. It may desensitize you toward poor morals and principles.

Engage with friends or acquaintances that are good for you and have good character so that you avoid conversations or behaviors that would corrupt your mind and soul. Your friends or acquaintances should also be honest with you and help affirm your good character. Those that "suck up" to you may cause your pride and ego to be overinflated.

Exercise to stay healthy. Exercise also causes the release of endorphins which can help alleviate stress, anxiety and depression.

Games are another possible means of relaxation. Games should be a diversion but if they turn into an activity that occupies too much of your thoughts, then it is no longer relaxing and can be detrimental, even addictive.

This rule has several key recommendations for living well, and balancing your personal life as compared to your work life. Everyone's work-life balance is specific to them. Only you can determine what the right amount of work and personal time is for you.

Here is a twist on a frequently advocated method of managing stress and anger levels. The common practice advocates that when you get angry, count to ten so that you can calm down some before responding in anger. However, instead of counting to ten, why not spend those same ten seconds or so praying about the situation? Prayer is powerful. Not only can God help you with your stress, but He can help you better manage your business. The Bible says to pray without ceasing. How much better our jobs would be if we prayed about everything!

Do you eat lunch at your desk so that you can continue working? If you work through lunch, then you may be allowing the stress to continually build up. You should consider that lunch can be a break away from the stressors of work. You may need to leave your workplace completely to escape the stress. For example, eating in a breakroom may leave you exposed to employees still seeking you out to discuss work matters. Leaving your work area will better allow you to take your mind off work and relax a little. Similarly, taking breaks throughout the day will need to happen in such a way that you can disconnect for a few minutes. Changing the environment can help to relieve stress. For example, having a One-on-one Meeting with your employee while taking a walk outside may improve the experience for both of you. Or alter your work hours, working early some days but only if you will also leave work early to spend time with family or other relaxing activities. Another consideration, when you are heading home try to leave your work at work because we need to have time to relax and time to spend with our family. There are many other activities that help reduce stress, and what works for others may not be what works best for you.

It is interesting that more than two centuries ago the business leaders specifically discussed relaxation. It is also interesting that they mention entertainment that is healthy and uplifting. After a rough day at work, it is easy to drop into the recliner and watch television that is less than enriching. The content on television today is often the opposite of uplifting and healthy, and the more we watch the more desensitized we can become. What I considered immoral just a few short years ago seems to have become more and more acceptable. We may rationalize that this is just realistic television programming. But do we allow the same lines to blur in our business dealings whereby what was unethical several years ago might be okay today? The world constantly and subtly invites us to drift away from the path that God calls us to follow. Drifting off the path God chose for us will add stress to our lives or possibly rob us from a more rewarding and joy-filled life! It is important to live a healthy and honorable life, but it is not easy to follow God's path in today's world. Hobbies may be a fun and healthy outlet for relaxation and entertainment, and we can choose from endless possibilities. However, these can also be destructive if allowed to become an obsession or in some cases even an addiction.

CALLED TO MANAGE

To better live a healthy and honorable life, we should associate with friends that are also of good character so that we do not get pulled into questionable behaviors. Have you ever had a friend who was less than a positive influence on you? When I was thirteen, my best friend would get drunk before school using the alcohol from his dad's liquor supply. When the supply dwindled he changed over to sniffing glue and aerosols, then graduated to marijuana and later "dropping acid." By the time we were fifteen, he was the main drug supplier in our school. Because I abstained from using drugs, I was not welcome in his new circle of friends. Being ostracized from this group was the best thing that could have happened to me, because most teenagers are pressured into drinking alcohol or taking drugs from the friends they associate with. As adults we may not succumb to peer pressure as easily (because we still do at times), but our friends still have an influence on us either directly or by association. Choose friends wisely, those that uplift and make you better. This is a great reason to be part of a Christian accountability group that meets regularly. We live in our challenging world and need God's support. Support that can be found through Christian support groups.

Many people make a "New Year's Resolution" regarding their health and their plans to "get into shape." As a result, exercise is the common plan to accomplish their goals. Even though very few usually succeed in their resolutions, exercise is still very important to one's physical and mental health. Research the endless possibilities of excise regimens to choose from and find one that works for you.

Games and gaming can be very relaxing, but games involving gambling may not be a stress reliever. Gambling with more than an insignificant amount of money may bring stressors to other areas of your life. Similarly, many other activities can become an obsession and even an addiction, impacting your physical, mental, emotional, and spiritual health. It can be destructive to families and to a person's financial health.

We need relief from the stresses of our work life, and entertainment, friends, hobbies and other activities can be very beneficial in releasing our stress. Find what works for you.

Rule 16: BE CONTENT WITH WHAT YOU HAVE
Be happy with what you have but continue to work diligently to improve your circumstances. If you do not achieve the success you work for, or are impacted by adversities of life, know that God is in control.

"Not one sparrow falls to the ground without your Father's consent." Matt. 10:29b (GNT)

"My punishment was good for me, because it made me learn your commands." Psalms 119:71 (GNT)

Focus on this content as well as other wisdom and scripture for a better understanding.

In whatever your circumstances, conduct yourself with patience, godliness and honor, focusing on your eternal life.

CALLED TO MANAGE

Why are you a manager, is it the power, the money, the status? These aspects may be very important to you, but there is a cost on your life, or more specifically on your soul. As you mature in your faith and gain wisdom these desires will become less important, but they will not go away. You will continue to struggle with them, but please know that you are not alone in facing these temptations. Lean on God, continue your faith journey and one day you will be perfected in eternity. Are you living your best life?

> *"Do not store up riches for yourselves here on earth, where moths and rust destroy, and robbers break in and steal. Instead, store up riches for yourselves in heaven . . . For your heart will always be where your riches are."* Matthew 6:19-21 (GNT)

Do you take time to count the blessings in your professional career? Whether you realize it or not, you are abundantly blessed in your professional career. Focusing on growing and developing other individuals can be a role that is extremely rewarding. Therefore, the most important objective should not be about making money or attaining more professional success. It is about doing the right thing for the people that work for you, the people that depend on you, the people whom you are accountable to. All of us are called to serve God and serve our neighbor, which for managers means serving your direct reports.

CALLED TO MANAGE

My prayer is that you find new knowledge or wisdom in this book, knowing that all knowledge and wisdom comes from God. As faithful stewards seek to serve God in all your endeavors, and He will bless you. Amen.

"God is the same Lord of all and richly blesses all who call to him." Romans 10:12b (GNT)

CALLED TO MANAGE

Appendix: Rules in Olde English

Rule I
Whatever you at any time intend to do, consider the end which you therein propose to yourself, and be sure that it be always really good, or at least innocent. He who does anything, and knows not why or wherefore, acts foolishly: And he who aims at an unlawful end, acts wickedly, which is the worst sort of folly. If you are careful always to observe this fundamental rule, you will thereby avoid many sins which would disturb your conscience, and also many trifling actions which would tend to your discredit, or perhaps trouble your repose.

Rule II
When you have thus fixed upon a proper end to aim at in each action, then consider not only what are the lawful means to be used in order to this end, but also how, and in what manner, these means are best to be applied and made use of. That which is unlawful ought not to be done, even for the obtaining of a good end: And means, in themselves good, have often failed of success, for want of prudence in the management of them.

Rule III

When you are seeking for a good end, proper means, and the right way of using them, remember that the knowledge of all this must not rest In idle speculation, or plausible discourse, but ought to be effectually reduced to practice, as often as you have an opportunity for it. That man who thinks wisely, and discourses judiciously, is never to be excused, If his practice, when there is occasion for it, is not answerable to his thoughts and words.

To him that knoweth good, and doeth it not, to him it is sin - James 4:17

And that servant who knew his Lord's will, and prepared not himself, neither did according to his will, shall be beaten with many stripes - Luke 12:47.

SUMMARY:

Take the sum and substance of these three rules In short let the end you aim at be always good. Be vigorous in making use of the proper means for the compassing of such an end. And in doing this be always very circumspect. If you proceed after this manner, you will certainly obtain the great end you propose to yourself in the life to come and if you fall short of some things which you desire in this world, you will have this comfort, that God thinks fit to deny them to you, not for any fault of yours, but for other good reasons, which he knows, though you do not.

CALLED TO MANAGE

Rule IV
Since our life here is short and uncertain, and the pleasures of it are always intermixed with doubts, fears, and sorrows of one kind or other; and since after it there a life to come which is to last to eternity ; a wise man will never propose the joys, pleasures, or prosperity of this transitory world, as the ultimate end of all, or indeed of any of his actions; but will always look beyond it, and make it his great business to secure his happiness In that other life, upon which he must soon and unavoidably enter.

O that they were wise, that they understood this, that they would consider their latter End! - Deuteronomy 32:29

So teach us to number our days that we may apply our hearts unto wisdom - Psalms 90:12.

Eternity is an end beyond which there can be nothing: And therefore whilst we have time, we ought to make due provision for it. This being the only true Wisdom.

Rule V
Since death is the only unavoidable passage into eternity, a wise man will make it the constant business of his life that he may die well, and that death may prove to him a passage not into eternal misery, but into everlasting happiness. Whoever is careless of this, it had been much better for him never to have been born.

Rule VI
The only sure way thus to die well, and at peace with God, is to live well. It is a foolish thing to rely upon what is very improperly called a death-bed repentance, to which God has made no promise. Repentance consists In a reformation of life; and what an absurd thing is it for a man to pretend to reform his life, when life itself is just at an end.

Rule VII

To live well is to be constantly obedient to God's commands, and never willing to do or desire any thing that is contrary to any of them. And in order to this you must be careful to know what these commands are, and to form a right notion of every one of them, without which you cannot give due obedience to them. For which reason, if you have had the advantage of a good education, it is your duty to make yourself thoroughly acquainted with the Holy Scriptures, where all God's commands are plainly recorded and set forth. If you are wholly illiterate, it is then your duty to make the best enquiry you can, what are the several things which God, your supreme Lord and judge, requires from you.

Whatsoever things are true, whatsoever things are honest, whatsoever things are just, whatsoever things are pure, whatsoever things are lovely, whatsoever things are of good report; if there be any virtue, if there be any praise, think on these things - Phil. IV. 8.

Rule VIII

Arm yourself, and often beg of God to arm you, with a fixed and firm resolution, that neither hope, nor fear, nor shame, nor hatred, nor love of any person or thing, shall at any time prevent you from doing what you know to be your duty, or prevail with you to commit what you know or believe to be a sin. Reason is the rudder wherewith you are to steer your course, and religion the compass by which you are to guide it: but resolution is the wind that will set you forward, without which your sails will often flag. Every morning therefore beg of God to instill this resolution into you, and often renew it in the course of each day.

Fear not them which kill the body, but are not able to kill the soul: But rather fear Him, who is able to destroy both soul and body in Hell - Matthew 10:28

Whosoever shall be ashamed of me, and of my Words, in this adulterous and sinful generation, of him also shall the Son of Man be ashamed when he cometh in the glory of his Father with the holy angels - Mark 8:38

I have sworn, and I will perform it, that I will keep thy righteous judgments. Psal.119:106

We ought to obey God rather than men - Acts 5:29

Rule IX
Let your light so shine before men, that they may see your good works, and glorify your Father which is in Heaven - Matthew 5:16.

But take not praise to yourself of any thing which you do.

Not unto us, O Lord, not unto us, but unto thy Name give glory - Psalms 115:1

Who maketh thee to differ from another? and what hast thou that thou didst not receive? Now if thou didst receive it, why dost thou glory as if thou hadt not received it - 1Corinthians 4:7

To deserve the love and good-will of those who know you, may well be a satisfaction, and in many case, of use to you. But the praise of men is an empty bubble, and so far from being of any real benefit, that it serves only to puff up those who are fond of it with pride and vanity, and thereby make them odious to God, and despicable in the sight even of those who praise them.

Rule X
Take care to fix right principles well in your mind; for want of which men are often inconsistent and unsteady in their actions, and uneasy to themselves and others. And when you have well fixed your principles, be sure always to speak and act according to them; and never to vary from them for the sake of party, or any other worldly consideration. For thus doing, God, your own conscience, and good men, will approve you: And you ought not to be moved at the censures of fools or wicked men.

Rule XI

Whatever you do or speak, let it always be done in its proper order, and in a suitable manner. Let that which of the greatest importance be first taken care of.

Seek ye first the Kingdom of God and His righteousness - Matthew 6:33

Let serious things be spoken and done seriously. Let good and friendly offices be performed with charity and good will, not grudgingly or of necessity. And the like may be said of all other your words and actions, which, when they are not only good, but also suitable to the importance which they do, or ought to carry in them, are pleasant to be seen and observed. But when there is a disagreement between the thing spoken or done, and the manner of speaking or doing it, it becomes more or less offensive, and sometimes ridiculous.

Rule XII

Be in reality what you are willing to be thought to be. Every man desires to be thought honest, just, and virtuous, that thereby he may gain love and good-will from all that know him. Now the only sure way to be thought so really to be so. Hypocrisy may for a while deceive the world; but in a little time it will be detected, and render an hypocrite odious to men, as he always is to God.

Rule XIII

Be in charity with all men; that is, fill your heart with a sincere love for all mankind, friends, strangers, and even enemies, if you have any. If you cannot always do this for their sakes who are of the same nature with you, yet do it for the sake of God your Creator, who commands it; and of Christ your Redeemer, who whilst we were yet sinners, and thereby enemies, died for us. Root out from your mind all envy, malice, hatred, and all ill nature. These are the storms and tempests of the soul, and the chief causes of all the disturbances in the world.

Let all bitterness, and wrath, and anger, and clamour, and evil speaking be put away from you with all malice. And be ye kind one to another, tender hearted forgiving one another even as God for Christ sake hath forgiven you - Ephesians 4:31-32

Particularly never be angry with a man and much less hate him, for being a different persuasion from you in matters of religion.

The Servant of the Lord must not strive; but be gentle unto all men, apt to teach, patient. In meekness instructing those that oppose themselves - 2 Timothy 2:24-25

In many cases you innocently may, and sometimes, you ought, by lawful means to defend yourself from an injury. But never do or say any thing beyond what is necessary for your own just defence or by way of revenge.

For vengeance is the Lord's and he will repay it. Be not therefore overcome of evil, but overcome evil with good - Romans 12:19 & 21

Scarce any man is capable of hating another, who, he finds, sincerely loves him.

CALLED TO MANAGE

Rule XIV
Affability and innocent cheerfulness in conversation, very much tend to maintain goodwill and agreement among those who converse together. Let it therefore always be your case, in whatever company you are, that your discourse, in your turn, be rational, easy, and inoffensive. Abstain from all biting and satyrical jest, and speeches, which will be remembered by others, when they are forgotten by you. There is no man but will take it to be set in an odious or ridiculous light, although it be but in sport.

Rule XV
Be always ready, according to your power to relieve the poor, and help the distressed. This will give great delight to your own mind, and gain you the good-will of all that know you. Remember the fortune you enjoy is not your own, but God's. He is the proprietor, you are only the steward of it, and must one day give a strict account of your stewardship. If therefore in your accounts, there may be many large articles of things that are unnecessary, and might have been spared, and but a few small ones for the relief of the poor, the fatherless, and the widows, can you ever hope to receive the reward of a faithful steward or servant?

CALLED TO MANAGE

Rule XVI
Be well content with your own condition, whatever it be. Endeavour by honest labor and industry, to make your circumstances better than they are, for the good both of yourself and others. But If such your endeavors do not meet with success, or if heavy afflictions bear hard upon you, remember that God governs the world by a particular providence.

That a Sparrow does not fall to the ground without Him - Matthew 10:29

That whom the Lord loveth be chasteneth and scourgeth every son whom he receiveth; that it is good for us to be afflicted that we may learn his statutes, Psalms 119:71.

Remember all this, and more that might be added both from reason and Holy Scripture, to the like purpose. Bear your afflictions patiently, and make the right use of them, and hope for a blessed reward In the life to come.

Rule XVII
Engage yourself in no more business than what you find yourself able to go through with. The want of this caution has made the life of many a man uneasy and unhappy, and involved his family and friends in numberless troubles and perplexities.

Rule XVIII
Meddle not with the affairs of any other man, which do not belong to you, except it be at his own desire to do him a charitable or friendly office; and this without doing any manner of wrong to another. It is a very unacceptable thing be a busy-body in other men's matters, either by word or deed.

Therefore study to be quiet, and do your own Business - 1 Thessalonians 4:11

CALLED TO MANAGE

Rule XIX
Engage not in any party-quarrels (whether public or private) any farther than the laws of God or your country oblige you, lest you be crushed between them.

Exercise yourself to have always a conscience void of offence toward God and toward men - Acts 24:16

This will give you quietness in your own mind, and the fault will not be yours if you are not at Peace with all men; which will be a great satisfaction to you.

Rule XX
Fly from the first [indication] of every temptation to sin; and take sanctuary in good thoughts, good books, or good and virtuous company. The surest way to keep yourself pure and unspotted, is to fly from temptation. If you cannot fly from it, call God to your assistance, and arm yourself with a firm resolution to resist it; and always be upon your guard, that you be not surprised.

Watch and pray, that ye enter not into temptation, the spirit indeed is willing but the flesh is weak - Matthew 26:41

It is much [easier] not to be wounded, then afterwards to be healed with a scar left behind; and to keep your enemy at a distance, than to engage with him when the victory is uncertain.

Rule XXI
Lead not an idle life, but be constantly employed in some honest business, whereby you may do good both to yourself and others. Idleness will betray you into many evils and inconveniences: for the spirit of man is of an active nature, and rather than be altogether idle, will be apt to employ itself in that which is evil. Nor does a man ever be more open to temptation than when he has nothing at all to do. If therefore you would keep yourself innocent, you must be careful to keep yourself always employed. For, besides that idleness would prove a snare to you, it is a shame and a sin, when there is so much of God's work to be done in the world, that any man, who pretends to be his servant should stand still, and not put his helping hand towards carrying it on.

Rule XXII
Be not slothful in business - Romans 12:11

For that is much the same with idleness, and sometimes worse than it. But when you have a firm prospect of doing what is good and rightly understand the ways and means of performing it, go on with resolution until you have completed it. You may possibly be sometimes defeated in a good purpose, but it is your duty to attempt it whenever you find a reasonable probability of success.

Rule XXIII
When you find yourself well able to do a good thing without the assistance of any one but God, never put it or any part of it off to be done by any other man, of whose honesty, sufficiency and industry you cannot be so sure, as in such a case, you may be of your own. But if you find that you want the help of others, let not the vanity of having all the praise to yourself make you decline it; lest the good you aim at may thereby be lost.

Rule XXIV

When you find yourself able to perform a good work today, do not put it off till tomorrow. Many a good undertaking has failed by unnecessary delay.

Thou knowest not what shalt be on the morrow, nor what a day may bring forth - James 4:14

Therefore whatever thy hand findeth to do, do it with thy might - Ecclesiastes 9:10a

Lawful gain may and ought to be made of the business which you engage in for without this, few men would be able to support themselves and their families, or do much good to others. But greediness after gain is a mischievous thing.

They that will be rich fall into temptation and a snare, and into many foolish and hurtful lusts, which drown men in destruction and perdition, for the love of money is the root of all evil - 1 Timothy 6:9-10

Among other qualifications of a righteous man, this is one;

That he despiseth the gain of oppressions - Isaiah 33:15

That is to say, all gain but what is just and honest. Gain a very strong temptation, against which therefore you must be very watchful, and upon your guard.

Rule XXV

If very much business unavoidably comes at once upon you, be not discouraged, for that will make you negligent, but consider how to put it in the best order, that one thing may be done after another, or without hindering each other.

Rule XXVI
Be always a good manager of your time, and lay hold of each opportunity that offers, for the doing whatever is necessary to be done. If you neglect a proper opportunity you may not perhaps meet with it again, whereas by dexterously laying hold of it, whenever it offers, you will be able to dispatch much business in a little time, and if you've accustom yourself to rise early, you will find that you have time enough to do the all the business that you have to do; and much more than persons who rise late will think possible to be done.

Rule XXVII
Always consider the probable consequences of what you intend to do; that you may guard against those that are evil or inconvenient. A thing may at first sight look very plausible, but If you look well to what may follow from it, you may find good reasons for laying It aside, or at least for altering your measures.

Rule XXVIII
Consult with yourself, and with others who are knowing and honest about everything of moment which you are to undertake, but waste not that time in unprofitable talk about it, which may be better employed in doing it. Thought is quick; and when a wise man is once well informed (of which he will take care) he not be long in deliberating what is best to be done. But many a good opportunity has been lost by too much consultation about it. A wise man thinks much, which is soon done, but speaks no more than what is necessary, being a good husband of his time, which is very precious.

Rule XXIX
Where you are not able to finish a business without the help of others call In speedily such persons to your assistance as are fit to be employed in it. The more hands are employed, the more work is done; provided they are managed in such good order, as not to be an hinderance to one another.

CALLED TO MANAGE

Rule XXX
Take some proper times to relax your thoughts from all business, that you may be better able to return to it. A heavy load constantly borne without any intermission, will waste your strength, and make you unfit for every thing. And at such seasons as these, divert yourself with reading some pleasant and innocent books, which at the same time may entertain and instruct you, without much labour or thought. But beware of all such books, poems, pictures, etc. as are profane, lewd, or debauched. These my well be compared to palatable poison. There may be wit in them, but if you read them they will insensibly corrupt both your morals and principles.

Or entertain yourself with a few agreeable friends, such as are social, good humoured, and sensible; whose conversation and behaviour may enliven your spirits, without the least danger of corrupting your heart. But shun flatterers, who, for some little ends of their own, will sooth and encourage you in every thing you say or do, whether It be right or wrong.

Or use moderate exercise, of such kind as is most agreeable to you, most suited to your constitution, and most conducive to your Health.

Or there may be no harm in sometimes amusing yourself at any of the customary games of chance and skill, with an agreeable friend or two. But never play for any thing that is considerable, or more than you or your friend may win or lose without any manner of concern. Remember it is designed to be a diversion, not business. If it employs too much of your time or thought, or provokes your passions, it changes its nature, loses its end, and ceases to be innocent.

Rule XXXI

At all times keep your passions under your command. Let them ever be guided by your reason, but never be a guide to it. Like fire and water, they are good servants but very bad masters. And if you suffer them to lead your reason, they will often betray you to say and do such things, as will hurt yourself, disoblige your friends, create you enemies, and expose you to scorn and contempt.

Rule XXXII

Take care of your health, for the sake of your relations and dependents, as well as for your own sake: and for that reason, as well as upon a principle of conscience, be strictly sober and temperate in eating and drinking. Intemperance is the cause of many diseases. Sickness is always a melancholy condition; but most of all so, when it is caused by a man's own irregularity or intemperance.

Rule XXXIII

Be very cautious what sort of friendships and acquaintance you contract. The character and success of your whole life in a great measure depends upon it. Become not familiar on any account with ignorant, empty, or vicious persons, from whom you can learn nothing but vice or folly.

Enter not into the path of the wicked, and go not into the way of evil men: Avoid it, pass not by it, turn from it, and pass away - Proverbs 4:15

But endeavour as much as you can, always to keep company with men of the best reputation for integrity and knowledge in their respective stations and callings. Associating with such persons will be of real service to you, establish your credit in the world, and contribute to your improvement both in wisdom and virtue.

CALLED TO MANAGE

Rule XXXIV
Be disposed to comply with all the innocent customs and manners of the place where you live, and the company that you keep, as far as you can with prudence: But be sure that they are innocent; and follow not a multitude to do evil. Remember that you are a Christian, and be neither ashamed nor afraid to speak and act like one upon all occasions.

Be ready to give an answer to every man that asketh you a reason of the hope that is in you - 1 Peter 3:15

Neither affecting to be thought a saint, nor dreading to be deemed a hypocrite by any man for so doing. But be not fond of entering Into debates about controverted or mysterious points of religion, of which you may be wholly ignorant without any hazard of your salvation. Such disputes often do great harm, and seldom do any good.

Rule XXXV
Have God in all your thoughts; study to know and do his will, and be instant in prayer to Him, through the mediation of our Lord Jesus Christ, for the assistance of his Holy Spirit to preserve and direct you.

Bibliography

Maslow, Abraham. "A Theory of Human Motivation" *Psychological Review* 50 (1943): 370-396. Print.

Some rules for the conduct of life: to which are added, a few cautions, for the use of such freemen of London, as take apprentices. London: printed by Henry Fenwick, [1800?]. Print.

www.ingramcontent.com/pod-product-compliance
Lightning Source LLC
Chambersburg PA
CBHW070638220526
45466CB00001B/226